FIELD NOTES

FROM A

PANDEMIC

ALSO BY ETHAN LOU

Once a Bitcoin Miner:
Scandal and Turmoil in the Cryptocurrency Wild West

FIELD NOTES FROM A PANDEMIC

A JOURNEY THROUGH A WORLD SUSPENDED

ETHAN LOU

SIGNAL

MCCLELLAND
& STEWART

Signal and colophon are registered trademarks of
Penguin Random House Canada Limited.

Library and Archives Canada Cataloguing in Publication data is available upon request.

ISBN: 978-0-7710-2997-4
ebook ISBN: 978-0-7710-2998-1

Cover design by Matthew Flute
Cover image: Nicki Pardo / Getty Images
Typeset by M&S, Toronto
Printed and bound in the U.S.A.

Published by Signal,
an imprint of McClelland & Stewart,
a division of Penguin Random House Canada Limited,
a Penguin Random House Company
www.penguinrandomhouse.ca

1 2 3 4 5   24 23 22 21 20

献给
爷爷

CONTENTS

PROLOGUE

Before I left for my travels, a trusted friend, a man of few words, all of which nonsense, offered practical advice. "Don't die," he said. I'm glad I listened. I did write a fair bit, though.

In times of crisis, I like to think, we are pared down to our most basic parts, our core functions. I am a journalist. I observe and I document. I scribbled from the field. I wrote from train cabins and airport benches and government-imposed quarantine, from an address once occupied by the composer Mozart's cousin.

It may or may not be relevant that I was born in China, although my family moved to Germany a year later, and then to Singapore before ending up in Canada, where I still live and work. While Toronto is my home base, I have written for international news organizations and have spent a lot of time travelling. I like to think I'm comfortable being anywhere—within reason, of course. This particular trip was certainly not one I had any intention of writing about. In fact, it was a trip to decompress after finishing another book altogether. I was to return to all the places I'd known and lived

—and more. I could not have foreseen the eventual upheaval and chaos of COVID-19—few could, most experts included. Even after being in China, my first stop, I expected other countries to remain unaffected. Then, as I moved on, I would look over my shoulder to see the plague had followed.

COVID-19 (coronavirus disease 2019) most likely originated in bats, moved on to other animals, and then crossed into the humans that handled them in a so-called wet market selling fresh meat and fish. The first cases—detected in Wuhan, Hubei province—resembled lung infections and were reported to the World Health Organization on New Year's Eve, 2019. Most people infected experience mild to moderate symptoms and do not require much, if any, treatment. Some may not even know they have it. But the elderly, and those with underlying issues such as diabetes, respiratory diseases, or cancer, often become seriously ill and even die. Experts quickly developed vaccines for trial, but they basically knew nothing about this novel coronavirus in the beginning. Suffice to say, there is still a lot we don't know about the virus and how it works, this tiny, thorny sphere of genetic material, a hundred million of which can fit on the head of a pin.

What we do know, without question, is the devastation in its wake, and the deep foreboding within that it will change life as we have known it. Six months after COVID-19 was discovered, what began in a market in China's ninth most populous city has already spread to nearly every country, with almost nine million cases and half a million deaths. At the root of such ongoing meltdown, mayhem, and lockdown—the virus spread through droplets, expelled by those infected in a sneeze or cough or even, as research suggests, in just their exhaled breath. Death hovered through the air, each and every one of us a potential agent for an enemy we could not see.

Despite evoking parts of history, this pandemic is different from everything we've seen in the past. Our world is more tightly integrated than ever, yet we were caught so unprepared and divided. We have become good at avoiding world war and nuclear destruction. Then along came an infected bat, and everything escalated with alarming speed and tenacity. The virus wiped away public life, eroded civil liberties, and decimated economies. It dealt distrust. And so, it will feed frustration and fear. It will stoke nationalism and fuel authoritarianism. It will upset long-standing balances of the world. While this is a travelogue of sorts, it is also about how everything we know will be changed by this thorny, microscopic sphere, and how the decisions made now, or indecisions, will shape and define the world for decades.

It all began—for me, at least—on January 23, 2020, two days before Chinese New Year, the Year of the Rat.

PART ONE
YEAR OF THE RODENT

I

The COVID-19 plague was already in the news when I left for Beijing from Toronto. But there was another knowledge within me, rumbling no less uneasily: my grandfather in China was dying. He had worsened so much in the past year, my father had once told me to "prepare a dark suit." For one reason or another, I had already delayed going to see him, and I could not put it off any longer. There was no question in my mind about this.

The trip to China was also to be the first leg of a long vacation around the world, for I had just finished the torturous task of writing another book, which is about the strange and complicated world of Bitcoin. I had planned more than a dozen stops, some for the sights, some to see friends and other family, for mine are scattered. I usually fly trans-Pacific once a year. This, though, was definitely one of my bigger trips. It had been in the works for months, meticulously planned. The bar for postponing it was high, and it hadn't quite been reached.

This was all back in January of 2020. The World Health Organization had not yet declared a global emergency. No travel restrictions were imposed, no lockdowns in place. The morning I left, an email news-letter I subscribe to had just two lines and one cartoon about what was then an odd little phenomenon that hadn't even been officially named. To be sure, I was far from unmoved—the shadow growing in the East and the first whispers of what may come; a novel strain of the coronavirus from China that causes breathing difficulties and is poten-tially fatal—I'd seen it before, a more lethal version. I lived through the SARS epidemic in Singapore. But while I've never forgotten, I also no longer feared.

Then I cleared Chinese immigration.

At Beijing's airport, the baggage-claim exit leads to an unusually lengthy barricade blocking the way. To get fully land-side, you have to walk past a long line of people, all crowding around the barrier, waiting to receive travellers. While I'm no stranger to this sight— they scan your face, you scan theirs, searching for recognition—this time, all I saw was a surreal wall of face masks, on and on, as far as the barricade stretched. With not one nose or mouth on display, it was like the sea of Guy Fawkes masks in V for Vendetta. They were eerily expressionless, yet almost starkly projecting a dark message I would only later learn.

It was two days before Chinese New Year. A lot can happen when you're in the air for fourteen hours without Internet. In that time, the Chinese government had taken the unprecedented step of sealing off the entire epicentre of the virus, the central city of Wuhan. The announcement was made just hours before it took effect. Eleven mil-lion people were locked in, the healthy along with the sick. The death toll was then seventeen. A woman from Wuhan, quoted in the news, posted on Chinese social media, "Now we are lambs who will still be slaughtered, and we can only leave our fates to the heavens."

I was supposed to meet my parents at the airport, who had flown in from Singapore, where they live. They didn't want my uncle in Beijing to make more than one trip to pick us up, so they suggested we book our flights to arrive in the city at around the same time. My parents like to be efficient, something I had definitely inherited. It likely manifested in the way I had planned this very trip, arranging all the stops in as straight a line as possible.

When I finally came to where they were standing, I almost didn't recognize my own parents. They too were in face masks, and after we embraced, so was I, for they immediately handed me one. It was the first time I ever wore such a veil, a light-blue surgical mask that smelled oddly like a closet. When we met my uncle, my father's younger brother, I saw he had gone a step further with a superior version: a Honeywell H910V Plus. It was angular and had a mechanical-like vent. I envied him because, in such a mask, exhaled breath goes out only via the vent; it does not leak out the top to fog up the glasses, as was the case with my surgical version. Masks like the Honeywell had been increasingly hard to find in China, but my uncle is resourceful. The man has always been sharp and one step ahead.

We got into my uncle's black BMW and headed out of the airport. The first thing I noticed was that my uncle had given his navigation system an accent that approximated that of his and my father's hometown, Shijiazhuang. It is three hundred kilometres southwest of Beijing, in the Hebei province, which is some nine hundred kilometres north of Hubei, whose capital is Wuhan. My father, who grew up speaking

Mandarin with his hometown accent, views Shijiazhuang's Mandarin as a dialect—which, in China, is often a matter of opinion. The line between an accent and a dialect is blurry—as grey as the gulf between a dialect and a language, which is mostly defined by the latter's speakers having borders and an army. Hong Kong's Cantonese, a southern tongue, and the mainland's northern Mandarin, for example, are not mutually intelligible and are considered dialects. But I, a Mandarin speaker, can understand the speech from the family hometown just fine. To me, it's just Mandarin with a funny twang. The English equivalent is probably a thick Boston accent.

But that's not an exact comparison. Accent in China carries more political and socio-economic connotations than it does in North America. It is no coincidence that Mandarin the dialect is the same word as mandarin the bureaucrat. Long ago, Mandarin, China's now-dominant dialect, was known as *Guanhua*, "the language of the officials." Not exactly a majority tongue. Now it is called *Putonghua*, "the normal language." And in an almost Canada-sized country with just one time zone that is Beijing's, where internal-migration restrictions mean social mobility is often tied to birth, less-prestigious regional tongues mark a person more than they do in English. Most people code-switch. My aunt, who lived most of her life in Shijiazhuang, does not speak with a Shijiazhuang accent. My grandmother has a mild one. My Beijing uncle and Singapore-based father speak standard Mandarin most of the time, but always put on their hometown tongue when they are home, almost going out of their way to show their roots. My grandfather—my yeye—is the lone outlier. My uncle's navigation system evoked the old man vividly. I don't know if he does not want to or cannot shake the accent. All I know is my yeye has a regional twang so thick you could stuff a mattress with it.

My yeye was born in 1938, just a little after the Japanese invasion of China, when the last Qing Dynasty emperor still reigned as a puppet in the north. In primary school, he met my grandmother, who came from a considerably wealthier family that made its money producing preserved vegetables, or Chinese pickles. My grandmother was born a year earlier, and as a baby during the war, she once cried so loudly while the family was hiding from Japanese soldiers that the adults almost killed her to save the wider group. She eventually became a chemist, and my grandfather, the first Lou and the first person in his neighbourhood to go to university, ended up a college physics teacher. At home, he was a noted tinkerer, fixing all sorts of electronics in the house. It must have rubbed off on my father, who became an electrical engineer. It definitely rubbed off on me, who, as a child, was also a tinkerer and copied my grandfather in all sorts of ways, some more welcomed than others. I drew laughs for mimicking my grandfather's accent, but imitating the way he stripped wires with his teeth was a serious no-go with my parents.

To his children, my grandfather had been a strict disciplinarian, a reflection, perhaps, of China's Cultural Revolution erupting around them, a period of intellectual and economic stagnation, unrest, and violence. But my grandfather was also unusually open-minded for his generation, rarely interfering with his children's life choices and never expecting any financial upkeep from them. He didn't need it anyway. Both grandparents had good pensions. But my grandfather, a lifelong smoker, got to enjoy retirement for only so long. Beginning with a stroke in the 2000s followed by a botched angioplasty procedure meant to treat narrowing blood vessels, he had been steadily fading in both body and mind. For years, he could barely recognize anyone and hardly ever spoke or moved.

On Chinese New Year's Eve, staff at the seniors' home in Shijiazhuang took our temperatures at the door in the dark and gloomy lobby, the infrared thermometers aimed at our foreheads like guns. They also noted our personal details before letting us in. Face masks were mandatory, of course.

My grandparents live on the second storey of the residence, in a room with two hard beds and a spongy green floor. It was one of the better residences—pretty expensive, as I had been told. At eighty-three, my grandmother—short-haired, bespectacled, and always wearing red—remains spry and vibrant, living at the seniors' home only to accompany my grandfather. As we chatted, she rather relentlessly offered us fruit, chocolate, and chrysanthemum tea. She asked about my relationship status, and I deflected with trained skill. There was a little more white in her hair, but otherwise, I swear my grandmother gets younger every time I see her. I was shocked, however, by how much my grandfather had deteriorated.

It was one thing to hear about it from my father. Quite another to see it directly. Just a year ago, my grandfather could stand if supported, swallow mushy food, and even arm-wrestle me, although not particularly well. Now, my grandfather was too weak to even sit in a wheelchair. Or sit anywhere. He just lay in his white-metal bed. A catheter bag that hung near his foot swelled with urine in real time.

A ventilator tube pierced his neck, connected to a machine that hummed and heaved. His hairless limbs were leathery from a lifetime of wear, yet thin with disuse. I was caught rather speechless seeing him this way. It was a lot to pack into that short visit. We had scheduled for no more than half an hour. The plan had been to go back the next day for a full visit, but as we left, residence staff told us, "It's best you don't come anymore."

We didn't listen.

While we were there the next day, however, what had been a recommendation the day before became mandatory. The residence officially banned all visitors. In the short time I had with him, I held my grandfather's hand and wondered if this was the last time I'd see him. Then, both the director and deputy of the facility came to the room and said we had to leave. It was muted and unaggressive, not the same way, say, security would escort someone out of a mall. From the looks on their faces and the halting manner in which they gave me the news, I thought they felt bad for expelling me, the grandson who had travelled from halfway around the world. But that wasn't quite it. Rather, it was fear— cold and weighty, yet effervescent, more contagious than any virus. After all, they were the ones who had to stay as we left, and it was obvious, even then, that things were only going to get worse. Within that realization was another: if my family and I had arrived in China just a day or two later than scheduled, the whole trip would have been for nothing.

Our eviction from the home was disheartening, but also understandable and hardly surprising given the climate of fear that had quickly enveloped the area, in nursing homes especially. Aging weakens immune systems. Later, surveys showed that only 2.3 per cent of those in China died after getting the coronavirus, but among those age eighty and older, that figure was 14.8 per cent. A coronavirus outbreak would be a disaster for any residence of the type my grandparents were in. In that event, statistically, at least one in seven seniors would not make it past the winter. In the weeks to come, nursing homes across the world would similarly shut their doors, both to the outside and between residents.

Farther north in China, in the city of Harbin, somewhere near Russia, I have another pair of grandparents. In Chinese, we call them *waipo* and *waigong*, "external grandmother" and "external grandfather," because they are my mother's parents. Traditionally, once married, a daughter is considered to be part of the husband's family. Thus, I am not part of my waipo and waigong's. But for people who do not share a surname, we are particularly close. I was born in their city, where my parents met. My waipo, eighty-one, had handled my poopy diapers—ours might as well be a bond forged on the battlefield. She gets so excited when I visit, she talks for hours, and the exertion of that leaves her tired even into the next day. My waipo and waigong are lucky in that they are healthy enough to live alone, but while nobody likes to acknowledge it, they too are declining.

My waipo had finished breast-cancer treatment just weeks before the coronavirus outbreak. Her legs are bowed, and she had a bad fall some years ago. She doesn't move around easily. My waigong, eighty-seven and a university professor, still works, but he's a little slower and thinner every time I see him. Both also take an assortment of medication for the variety of random ailments you get as you age. My mother worried for her parents: With healthcare systems overwhelmed by the virus, who would take care of her parents' regular medical needs? What if they caught something at the hospital? What if they caught something at the grocery store? There was no choice but to shut out the world. And that's not a viable solution, especially for the aged, who often need ongoing medical care of one form or another. In New York, for example, when the crisis hit, media reported that the exacerbation of an overwhelmed healthcare system with the real fear people had of going to a hospital with anything but COVID-19 symptoms resulted in an untold number of deaths—from heart attacks, seizures, and other life-threatening conditions—that might have otherwise been prevented. One source of optimism, a straw of hope on which to grasp, was that even in isolation, my waipo and waigong had each other. They weren't handling this alone, like so many other older people.

The day after my family and I got evicted from the seniors' home, the second day of Chinese New Year, was traditionally the day married daughters are supposed to return to their maiden homes. My father's older sister, who still lives in Shijiazhuang, had planned to visit my grandparents at the seniors' residence, but that was obviously not an option anymore. Instead, our extended family had a hotpot lunch at my grandparents' former apartment, which was only a short distance from the seniors' residence. All their old furniture was still in place, but the home is only occupied when their faraway children visit. There, my father proudly showed us the little wooden chair he had insisted my grandfather buy for him because my aunt also had one. It still bore my father's name at the bottom.

With chopsticks, we dropped raw ingredients—thin beef and lamb slices, dumplings, mushrooms, vermicelli, and meat balls—into a communal pot of boiling abalone soup, eating as we cooked. I've always loved the sesame sauce we dip each bite into—particularly for its thickness. Because everything you eat in hotpot is fished out of the soup, the dipping sauce gets watered down quickly. The merit of any sesame sauce, I've always believed, lies entirely in its viscosity.

We also had garlic stems, sliced tofu, century egg—its flavour derived from hydrogen sulfide and ammonia, truly an acquired taste—and a sort of glutinous cake specific to Shijiazhuang, which only my father likes. We washed it down with a brand of lager called Snow. It was a glorious meal for everyone except my grandparents. At the seniors' home, my grandfather lay motionless in his bed. My grandmother could join us only via video call. Still, with my aunt's entire family present, my uncle, my parents and me, it was the closest thing to a reunion we had had in nearly fifteen years. My grandmother wasn't eating because it was before her scheduled time to do so, but she watched us through the entirety of the meal.

We left the city—an abrupt change of plans—not just because my grandparents were off-limits to us but also because, around the country, what had started as a sort of precautionary worry about the virus had morphed into a full-blooded, into-the-valley-of-death-rode-the-six-hundred alarm. The previous night, after ejection from the seniors' home, we heard some intercity passenger buses were being shut down. My uncle worried that private cars would soon be banned as well, more or less preventing us from leaving the city at all. My parents and uncle's plan had been to spend the whole week in Shijiazhuang. My plan was to spend two weeks there, seeing my grandparents, taking it easy. Now, it was off to Beijing. There, even amid a lockdown, my uncle figured we could still get to the airport at least, or that was the idea. Like everyone else, we were caught unprepared in a dramatic escalation of events over which we had no control. Nobody knew what was going on or what was about to happen.

2

Chinese New Year is based on the lunar calendar, the cycles of the moon. The exact date of the celebration is thus different every year, although it is usually in January or February, when the new year is marked by a new animal zodiac sign. Also called the Spring Festival, Chinese New Year is a bit like Asian Christmas, but like everything in China, it tends toward extremes, and not just because it's a country of 1.4 billion people. Over decades, the rapid development of urban centres had resulted in a mass of outward internal migration from rural areas, rich and poor, skilled and unskilled alike seeking better lives. China's post-Mao city population spike of hundreds of millions was called "likely the largest in human history" by one researcher. The very fact China restricts internal migration through its Hukou household-registry system points to people's doing it too much. The return home for the New Year thus represents a massive migration. The whole country is given a week-long public holiday. All sorts of travel tickets sell out quickly. The move to online systems for train tickets had been criticized for alienating migrant workers who might not be technologically savvy or even own a computer or smartphone. The New Year migration is the sort of journey that every Chinese person knows, a shared experience regardless of social class.

Going home for the festivities is such a big deal, the Chinese even have a word for it: *chunyun*. This year, before the Chinese New Year, the same as every other year, hundreds of millions of people left their cities of work for their hometowns. While those living elsewhere, like me, may not do so every year—in fact, this was my first time—anyone else with family in the old country has probably done it at least once. The annual migration almost defines Chinese identity, like a pilgrimage to Mecca. The fact that the virus happened during *chunyun* is a cruel joke; now, as hundreds of millions were planning on going back to their cities of work, many found they could not do so.

My uncle drove my parents and me back to his apartment in Beijing without issue. The government never did ban private car travel between cities as feared. But in other parts of the country, confinement and clampdown were seen like never before. At least fifteen more cities in Wuhan's Hubei province had some sort of travel restrictions imposed, bringing the total number of people locked down to more than 50 million. It felt, at the time, like the kind of thing that could only be possible in China, which has both the necessary resources and tight central-government control to carry out its will. Later, of course, it proved possible in many other countries too.

We might not have been in Wuhan itself, but things were only marginally better in Beijing. To leave your apartment, more often than not, you needed to register and get the equivalent of a permission slip from security. To an outsider, it may be unclear where the building management gets that authority. But this is China, where historically, the State owned and planned everything and the concept of private ownership was nonexistent. The post-Mao reforms have drastically changed that status quo, but the past lingers. For many people, their apartments are still tied to their employment. It remains a country where many things link back to the government. Beijing, densely urbanized, is also a city where few people live in single-family houses, and where even detached homes are usually part of some sort of gated compound. The so-called neighbourhood committees looking over these compounds are effectively extensions of the local authorities, which derive their power from the State. Big Brother is not exactly in your bedroom, but he's close by. I could only imagine what would have happened if one or all of us were from Hubei.

The restrictions on coming and going were a hurriedly assembled smattering of rules. It seemed to be a bottom-up effort by local officials to conform to what they thought the central government wanted. What worked for one apartment complex might not work for another. If you could drive, you could bypass the rules slightly, but licence plates, which got scanned at the gate, were still linked to personal details, and you still had to submit to a temperature check when you returned, just like when riding the subway or entering the airport. Sometimes, security at apartment complexes insisted drivers get out of their cars to get permission slips to leave as well, but they relented if you resisted.

In Beijing, restaurants were enforcing identification checks. At one eatery, the server told me they needed to know where we were coming from. Most Chinese identification cards—which everyone has—include hometown addresses, labelling people more explicitly than any accent. Chinese telecommunication companies later launched a feature that could generate a list of provinces recently visited, based on your phone number, which they track. Officials at a train station, for example, would demand passengers' location lists. If you were connected to the affected province, you were a leper of the second-class kind. One Hubei woman said, in a widely circulated social-media post, she had been rejected by more than ten hotels. Everything felt a little dystopian. China is where everything is recorded and linked to everything else, and there is only a faint shadow of the concept of personal privacy. The pandemic had brought all of that eerily to the fore, demonstrating just how much oversight the government has over its people. The Hubei woman eventually found accommodation, but only because the so-called Internet police quickly saw her post and intervened.

At the Beijing restaurant that checked our identities, my family and I had a main course of *zhajiangmian*, dark, soybean-paste noodles with slivers of pork belly, and a brownish stew of fatty pig intestines, noted for its slight sourness. A man at a table behind us had the same stew and a small bottle of domestic rice liquor. He was playing popular Chinese music from his phone and was obviously drunk, quickly becoming incoherent and rude to the waitress, although not to the point that it required intervention. He was the only other customer in the restaurant besides us, and the whole scene was just eerie and a little bit apocalyptic, considering the circumstances. That meal would turn out to be the last we ate outside of our apartment.

My parents left China three days later to return to Singapore, as scheduled. My uncle and I saw them to the airport, but we didn't get out of the BMW. I can't remember whose idea it was, but the rationale for remaining in the car was pandemic-related: the less interaction with strangers, the better. It was thus a subdued goodbye, said between car seats. My uncle and I did, however, stay in the BMW in the parking lot until my parents texted to say they'd cleared airport security and got to their gate. In these uncertain times, you never know what can happen.

I thought of changing my flight to leave earlier but decided against it. I was young, fit, and healthy. I hadn't seen a doctor in five years. I'd be departing in a week anyway, and I figured it wasn't worth the trouble.

I spent the days in my uncle's apartment, just the two of us. My uncle is married with two children, but both wife and kids are living in New Jersey, having more or less emigrated. My uncle remained behind to work, which isn't as uncommon as it may sound. Academics have a term for it: "astronaut families," in which one member endures separation, often not entirely by choice, to "maximize their earnings," as one geographer described it. My uncle is a lawyer in China, but—with laws unfortunately being tied to countries and whatnot—his career just isn't something easily transferrable to the United States. He is also a workaholic, and thus doesn't have a lot of downtime during which he can fly halfway around the world for a visit. He actually hasn't seen his family in person for years, which is, I admit, a little extreme, even by astronaut family standards. To make up for his physical distance, my uncle emails his children with life advice almost every day, both to exercise his paternal responsibilities and to practice his English. His emails read like philosophical essays, full of practical advice mixed with questions about life itself. While in Beijing, I helped him edit those emails, which added some levity to an otherwise dark situation. One of his essays was on the importance of brushing your teeth every day: "It was your parents' duty to give you a whole body; then after that, it is your turn to protect yourself from being destroyed—any part of it—or you would be handicapped, for even the lack of a single tooth makes you less whole." Needless to say, my uncle is known as the family eccentric.

Another email was about me, sparked by his fascination with my weathered and well-worn Clarks desert boots. It made me laugh, for it was accurate in a way that had never occurred to me. "Do you know whose leather shoes are in the attached picture?" my uncle wrote. *The owner is not a beggar. The owner is, in fact, your cousin Ethan. I read a book by Max Weber,* The Protestant Ethic and the Spirit of Capitalism, *in which the German sociologist attributes success to frugality and discipline. Austerity begets thrift and creation, which you will find in your cousin Ethan's personality,* "manifesting as . . . wearing a beggar's shoes."

And, of course, there were emails on the subject of COVID-19. *This current situation, this to-the-death duel with the virus particles, could have all been avoided,* he explained. "If we had left it where it should be, in the host bats' bodies, we would not need to face the serious choice: they die, or we die." *Humanity has encroached further and further into the wild, perhaps unwittingly violating a metaphysical equilibrium between species,* he reasoned. "If one of them is too powerful to co-exist with others, the chain will be broken, and nature will lose its balance. Some unpredictable result will appear."

When ants bite a dog, he suggested, *and the owner pours boiling water on the colony in retaliation, the insects die without knowing why:* "Due to being humble and menial, the ants could not know the function of boiling water, the relationship between the dog and his owner, as well as humans' power. We humans could decide their living or dying; thus, we are their God, who cannot be recognized by them." *Perhaps by eating bats, as some theories say, we did something to the pets of some higher intelligence, and we are being punished without knowing why,* my uncle wrote. "God decides to punish us by coronavirus, as we subject the ants to genocide."

My uncle didn't mean everything that seriously, of course. He made the bat–ant analogy only to illustrate a broader point about the need to "stand in awe of nature." My uncle is irreligious, and while in Beijing, he had told me that if I could find a stance for him to take—any position on any issue—then he could find the necessary reasoning and argument to defend it. He is that good of a lawyer, he said, "a sniper." He was, again, only being half serious when he said that.

I could only imagine what my cousins must have thought when they read the emails. Me—I had faithfully done my best to edit his missives, and to find meaning in them. He did raise a good point about the coronavirus—is there a reason this happened? Why now?

Perhaps the fact that this had to be asked—the fact that such a threat came so suddenly and caught us so ill-prepared—is a sort of answer in itself.

I spent the remainder of my time in Beijing catching up on some of my own work and reading. My uncle, who also teaches at a local university, worked too. The reopening of school had been pushed back, so he had more time to prepare for his classes. But his legal workload also increased: a client of his sold body-temperature-monitoring devices, of all things, and had fresh orders, so my uncle and his team were busy drafting contracts.

My uncle likened our experience to being in prison, and I took that as more than hyperbole, for the man had visited Chinese detention facilities many times to see clients. We left the condominium only in the evening to work out at the satellite campus of my uncle's university, near his apartment. The main campus had been closed. My uncle ran on the track, and I did chin-ups on a yellow bar caked in dust. There wasn't much else going on, for aside from a security person, I saw— fleetingly and separately—only one other person and three dogs idly hanging around. Of course, condo security checked our temperatures when we got back. Everyone screened for temperatures everywhere.

Then one day, as my uncle and I arrived on campus, we saw the university had closed the satellite compound and tripled security at the gate. My uncle turned the car around.

By then, early February, the world had more than 17,000 cases of the coronavirus, although 99 per cent of them were in China, where at least 360 had died. Beijing, which had more than 200 infected, had seen its first death a few days earlier.

I had originally wanted to see friends in the city but was uncertain about etiquette. This was before the concept of physically social distancing had entered the zeitgeist, when the world outside was still carrying on more or less as normal. Even then, though I was not consciously aware of it, I think I already had some sort of inkling of the seismic shift in societal culture that was to come. It wasn't so much the lockdown rules that were imposed but people's rapid unity in conforming to them; not just obeying the guidelines, but earnestly believing in them.

There are always outliers, of course, but in my social circle, at least, I would later find people isolating themselves more stringently than dictated by their governments and viewing those who did not negatively. Suggesting an in-person social meeting, or even just going outside unnecessarily or visiting grandparents, would be perceived as irresponsible and socially unacceptable—not just on the level of jaywalking or doing recreational drugs, more like not wearing a seat belt or driving while drunk. Germans, for example, stereotypically conformist, "zealously" reported people flouting physical distancing rules, as described by *Reuters*. As for my social life in Beijing, I felt a little uneasy at the time. It was like hearing distant thunder on a Sunday afternoon. If everyone was worried about contagion, would a message from a friend who had come from far away be perceived as an obligation, making people say yes to meeting up, but reluctantly? I erred on the side of caution and never told anyone I was in Beijing.

At the same time, there's a reason that waterfront properties are prized, that we have balconies, and that even the densest, greyest metropolises have little green parks. We are animals still. Like the orcas whose normally upright fins collapse in captivity, looking at walls and computer screens every day was chipping away at something inside me. On my last night in Beijing, I couldn't take it anymore. I had to be out in the world, to walk the streets, if only to see the sky and breathe the snow.

3

My way into the city, to downtown, was underground. If you've ever witnessed the chaotic human-traffic masses of the Beijing subway— which handled 10 million people a day, having built twenty-one lines in eighteen years—you'd certainly never forget the sight of it the evening I was there. It was a little after rush hour, but there were no more than a dozen people on any given train, even though, as the large transparent stickers on the windows assured us, the cars were disinfected every day. The Chinese term sounds harsh when translated literally—*xiaodu*, to "eliminate the poison." There was an eerie stillness, a nothingness in the air that said volumes.

There were red banners at the stations that read, "For the health safety of you and your family, please comply with temperature checks proactively." Strung across public places, such notices have been a part of government campaigns for decades in China, propagating official messaging and stances. With the coronavirus outbreak, those banners had become more threatening and harsh, which I guess is the whole point. In translating, I've painstakingly preserved the trademark rhyming scheme many of the slogans have:

"Mutual slaughter comes from going to a social gathering; seeking an untimely death is the resultant path of partying."

"A meal of wildlife today; in hell, tomorrow, you'll stay."

"If today you go outside to run around, next year, on your grave, growing grass will be found."

"Leaving the village is like committing suicide; the safest choice you can make is to stay inside."

"Broken legs if to go out you insist; shattered teeth if, verbally, you resist."

"To go outside without a mask providing facial coverage—that is not the behaviour of a human, but a creature of garbage."

The subway stations blared announcements, saying the surroundings were disinfected five times a day and that the metal detectors—to which everyone in China had to submit if they wanted to ride the subway, even before the virus outbreak—were disinfected once per hour; all staff must wear masks, and all customers were encouraged to do the same.

In the subway cars, the television screens cycled through virus-related news clips, anchors teaching viewers how to properly use face masks and celebrities in vertically oriented smartphone-filmed videos expressing support for China through this difficult time. Chinese media outlets in general were unnaturally co-ordinated, often depicting selfless medical workers or healed patients flush with gratitude. But there was almost nobody on the subway to watch them, except the blue-vested people whose job it was to stand by the doors. They also wore little red caps and matching armbands. "Customer service management personnel," they were called. In front of me, a cloth shopping bag, slightly soiled, was left on the seat.

I could see my masked reflection in the dark subway window. Before I'd left the apartment, my uncle had given me his last spare unused Honeywell H910V Plus face mask, a superior model to the surgical mask but strange looking by usual standards. I found myself vaguely creature-esque, like a *Harry Potter* house elf, for the mask had tight elastics, pulling my ears forward and outward. I felt as odd as I looked. A respiratory mask like the Honeywell forms a perfect seal around your nose and mouth, protecting against fine, airborne particles. The common surgical mask, on the other hand, is only a simple physical barrier, protecting against droplets. I had been wearing surgical ones for the entire time I was in China. Breathing with a respiratory mask no longer fogged up my glasses, but it felt harder than normal and uncomfortable in its own way. And my ears felt sore.

Pretty soon, I acclimatized to my respiratory mask. I forgot it was even there. I was fortunate that I didn't have to endure it for long sustained periods, but for many, such as doctors, service workers, and store clerks, it was required every day, all day. Weeks later, Singapore issued masks to every household and started handing out fines to anyone caught in public without one.

A few days earlier, someone sent me a picture of an Asian-looking man in Toronto wearing one of those heavy-duty chemical-warfare masks that covers the whole face. We had a good laugh at that guy and his paranoia. Then, while I rode the Beijing subway, I saw two people with the same mask. In the city, I even saw a child, no more than five years old, with an entire plastic sheet draped dangerously over his face.

Later, when I was sent pictures of people with water-cooler bottles over their heads or a little dog and its owner all bundled up in plastic, it didn't seem so funny anymore.

I couldn't quite appreciate the extraordinariness of the situation in Beijing until it literally stared me in the face. Perhaps it was because I'd been far away, where you don't exactly realize how painfully real things are. When my uncle gave me his last mask, I suspect it wasn't just out of concern for his favourite and only nephew. It was for his own interests, too. He didn't want to catch anything from me.

I probably shouldn't have gone out. After I got off the subway and started walking around the streets, what I encountered was only a husk of the city, a movie set, not real. It was hard to experience the joy of finally being outside the apartment because there really wasn't any life to see. Some shops had cut their hours, but most had shut down completely. The restaurant at which my family had eaten a week earlier, the one that checked our identification documents, was closed. Most shops that had been open just a week earlier were all shuttered. Some had printed signs, repeating the government line discouraging public gatherings. Some had only simple handwritten ones, saying, "Temporarily closed." Even the stores that stayed open closed early. Beijing's famous twenty-four-hour bookstore, Page One, had cut its hours to just seven. Yet it might as well have not opened at all, if the snow outside its entrance was any indication. It was an unbroken film of white, unblemished by footprints. In fact, the whole downtown was a sea of blankness, like an unfinished painting.

Outside Tiananmen Square, in the prime tourist area of the pedestrian-only Qianmen Street, aside from security and the workers sweeping away snow, there was no more than a handful of people milling around. Many of them were photographers, taking the chance to capture a rare empty Beijing. In some parts of the city, there were more policemen than civilians. There was absolutely nothing to do, and hardly a soul in sight. The traffic was sparse. At times, the only thing moving was the falling snow. There were tracks on the ground. People had clearly come and gone. But even the footprints were shallow, covered by the ice crystals soon after they were made; then nobody stepped over them again. No marks reached the dark ground itself. The parked cars and motorcycles also had thick layers of snow on them. What was normally one of the busiest places on Earth had become a desolate land. Farther away, the Forbidden City and sections of the Great Wall were closed. So was Shanghai's Disneyland—"The Happiest Place on Earth," as its slogan says.

Interestingly, the only places consistently open were the Western chain restaurants, which arrived in the country some thirty years ago, when China's previously closed economy opened up. These eateries have been the source of much polarization. My grandfather, older than both the People's Republic of China and the romanization used to spell his name in English, never did have a taste for them. A fan of fatty pig intestines, my grandfather had once told me of what he viewed as the gastronomical pointlessness of hamburgers and pizzas. That food is not for everyone, for sure. Nothing about them is very Chinese, even if they did adjust the menu slightly for local palates. Nevertheless, the chains have been wildly popular in China, pulling in $150 billion in 2017 and growing by 10 per cent every year. Those franchises were among the West's biggest cultural exports. They were both novelties and the sum and symbol of economic success. Their mushrooming—a new Starbucks every fifteen hours—was a microcosm of the rapid development that, for those like my grandfather, dramatically transformed the world around them in a way they never would have expected. Those fast food restaurants, many open twenty-four hours a day, have also provided shelter to the homeless and the drunk, rural people seeking their fortunes in the big city, and anyone who cannot afford a hotel room for the night—the so-called McRefugees.

A little beyond Tiananmen Square, I saw people huddled in a KFC, plugging in their phones and laptops. Not only was this the first of the American chain's restaurants in China, it was the first fast food eatery by any Western company to open in the country, launched about ten years after the founding father Mao Zedong's death. Now, it was one of the only places left for these people, who perhaps had nowhere else to go that night.

When I got to a nearby McDonald's, I bought a cup of hot bubble tea and sat down to remove my mask and drink it. Then the manager approached. She was slight, with a dyed pixie cut and a look about her that conveyed an odd mixture of weariness and uncertainty. Because of the virus, the restaurant was doing only takeout. Nobody was allowed to dine in, she said. "Young man, you'd better leave."

Outside, the moon glinted on the white frost, the lunar light shining through the overcast. The bubble tea was warm both in my hand and in my throat, steaming from the cup's lid and marking my exhaled breath prominently. That trip to downtown Beijing was like a season in itself, dark and daylong. I walked back in a world suspended, frozen between one snowflake and the next.

4

The snow fell through the night, out of darkness and into darkness. Beijing gets the flurries probably just a hair more than, say, the coastal and temperate Vancouver. China's capital thus doesn't deal with it well. Parts of the highway were still slick with snow on my way to the airport. My uncle had budgeted two hours for a half-hour drive, and he was wise to have done so.

My next stop was supposed to be Hong Kong to see my British friend Kevin. Eight years ago, we interned together at a little newspaper in Singapore that now no longer exists, having merged into another. It was only to be a short visit, but I had been looking forward to it, and to revisiting old times covering scandal, murder, and other assorted crimes and improprieties. But Kevin, who now writes for an aviation trade publication, was not in Hong Kong. He had been in the United States for vacation, and because of the coronavirus situation, he had decided to not go back to Hong Kong at all, instead joining his lawyer girlfriend, C.J., in Singapore. The couple lives and works in Hong Kong, but it is common for major companies, law firms, and banks to have offices in both financial hubs of Singapore and Hong Kong, and for their workers to split their time between the cities. C.J. is a Singaporean, and the couple's plan was to ride out the coronavirus storm—or part of it, at least—in a place where life was still normal. My route to Hong Kong, though, had already been planned, so I decided to go nonetheless.

I never ended up making it.

The runway was thick with snow, and it continued to grow thicker. I was supposed to transfer in the northern Chinese city of Dalian to get to Hong Kong, but in Beijing, the plane I was on was stationery for a good hour. Then we had to change planes, for the cold had broken the aircraft. I thought I was going to miss my connection but quickly discovered worse: all Air China flights from the mainland to its special administrative region were cancelled.

It had been a tumultuous time. After more than half a year of chaos—city-wide pro-democracy protests against the mainland Chinese government—the virus had hit Hong Kong like a sucker punch. I'd been quite plugged in to the situation there due to my work as a journalist. For a long time, there'd been some sort of protest happening somewhere in Hong Kong every day—and some sort of government response as well. The day before I left Beijing, I called Hong Kong's deputy director of information services, Brett Free—a former journalist originally from Australia—only to catch him right before a press conference. For a city mired in socio-political dissension, the virus had added a whole new level of volatility, the *Los Angeles Times* wrote. The Hong Kong government, whose name was already mud to many residents, had been catching fresh flak for its allegedly lethargic response to the virus and for not banning visitors from the mainland. In the face of this heat, on the day before I left Beijing, probably at the very press conference into which Free was heading when I called, Hong Kong announced quarantine measures for all visitors arriving from the mainland. They hadn't taken immediate effect, but flights were cancelled nonetheless. And not all travellers were given notice.

Some, like me, found out only at the Beijing airport. It was a good thing the cold delayed the first leg of my flight and then disabled the plane. Otherwise, I would have found out only at the Dalian airport, stuck in some random Chinese city to which I'd never been and about which I knew nothing. And Hong Kong was not the only destination to be so affected, I soon realized. Travel restrictions related to China had started to blossom around the world. All sorts of flights ended up cancelled. When I went to get my flight rerouted, I saw that a long queue snaked in front of Air China's re-booking counter, although any semblance of order quickly faded.

A Chinese woman, probably no older than thirty, was crying. "I waited at gate C30 for forever," she said. Whatever her problem was, she left the counter with it unresolved, still in tears. Another woman brazenly cut the queue, four Chinese passports in her hands and a flock of children waiting far behind. She was red-clad, with a look that was both determined and vulnerable at the same time. I did not have the heart to call her out. In front of the red woman, a group of male Kazakh students held up the line, fistfuls of Chinese yuan in their hands, but apparently not enough to get flights for all of them. "If we wait, would there be cheaper tickets?" one asked haltingly. The red-clad queue-cutter tried to help them, but it was of little use. The

Kazakhs spoke little Mandarin or English, although I did make out that they'd been at the counter for more than two hours.

At the counter beside the Kazakhs, a Chinese couple asked for flights out. "Any tickets to Toronto? Or Montreal? Or anywhere in Canada?"

Another man tried to go to Italy.

"Are you holding a Chinese passport?" staff asked.

"Yes, but Chinese people aren't banned. Only flights from China," he said. "I can go there if I fly indirect."

A Chinese woman, who had American permanent residency, wanted to go to New York. "I have a green card," she made sure to mention.

But none of that mattered. The counter couldn't book any flights to countries with travel restrictions, a staff member said. Everyone was in a face mask.

Eventually, 90 per cent of the Earth's population would live in countries with coronavirus-related travel restrictions. And the varieties of restrictions would become worse. Countries would go from rules specific to China to wholesale barring of non-residents unless a passenger had good reason to travel, whatever that meant. Canada, the European Union, you name it. Even North Korea. The United States would make a slew of immigration suspensions. Some countries, such as Namibia, would close their borders to even citizens unless "their mission is critical to national interest." Airlines around the world would ground their planes, stocks tumbling accordingly. The industry would quickly lose up to $314 billion in ticket sales, according to the International Air Transport Association. South African Airways eventually planned to close up shop, sell off all its assets and lay off all its staff. I was sure my friend Kevin, who reports on and for the aviation industry, would become a lot busier, but I also wondered who would be left to read what he writes. The entire concept of travel would be redefined. Within a few short weeks, the idea of going somewhere purely for the experience, to meet new people, to take in different cultures or just for a change of environment, a break—an idea that has defined the Western backpacking coming-of-age ritual, an idea that reflects the long arc of our history toward increasing interconnectedness—would be wiped away.

At the Air China counter, I was among the lucky ones. I was put on a 3 p.m. flight to Singapore, bypassing Hong Kong, just like Kevin. But it was definitely an ordeal. I had already gone through security and sat on a plane for a whole hour before finding out everything was cancelled. And even at the counter, I waited so long, my phone's battery died. I've never been much of a day drinker, but when I finally got to the Air China lounge, nearly ten hours after I had woken up that morning, the first thing I had was a Tsingtao beer.

Even there, in what is usually an oasis, an escape from the airport at large, there were signs that not everything was as it should be. The lounge had gotten rid of all its fine china. There were no ceramic mugs, no metal utensils. Everything reusable had been purged. But the sourcing for the disposable dinnerware was clearly improvised. Even in the first-class lounge—I got in only because of some special deal my credit card affords me—all the airline had were metallic takeout boxes and plastic cups so small it was hard to fathom what you were supposed to drink out of them. I got creative and made tea in one of the takeout boxes.

———

37

In Beijing, and then in the act of leaving China, I had a rare window into what had become a surreal and bizarre realm, an experience, first-hand, of how things got progressively worse, how in the face of the virus, restrictions on the way people lived their daily lives became increasingly heavy, their ability to see friends and family limited. But that experience was more than a gander at the problems of a faraway country. It was a sign of what was to come for the world—like the sharp smell of ozone before a lightning storm.

Soon, of course, it wasn't just China, as the virus spread. In nine days in March, U.S. president Donald Trump went from disregarding the crisis to saying he had "always treated" it "very seriously." In the same nine days, the Western world descended into panic-buying, economic meltdown, closed borders, lockdowns, and social isolation. Much of the European Union and North America would declare states of emergency in the coming weeks, with most people kept indoors. Italy, with remarkably high infection rates and death tolls, would implement among the most extreme measures. It was just like how, in fourteen hours in January, while I was in the air between Toronto and Beijing, an entire city had been sealed off.

Even though many governments would be accused of acting too late, when they eventually did, it was swift and with little warning. "Decisions that in normal times could take years of deliberation are passed in a matter of hours," wrote the Israeli historian and author Yuval Noah Harari. "Immature and even dangerous technologies are pressed into service, because the risks of doing nothing are bigger." One Chinese national in Singapore would have his permanent residency stripped after authorities said he disregarded a quarantine order, an unusual punishment meted out within three days of the alleged incident. Singapore would pursue aggressive contact-tracing, roping in the police and military to meticulously comb the movements of known carriers of the virus and any people with whom they came into contact. Non-co-operation would be made illegal. As a city-state without a big country's myriad levels of government, it could act quickly. In addition to making masks compulsory, Singapore banned all social meetings between people from different households and developed an app that recorded everyone with whom you came into contact. South Korea would follow comparable measures, underscoring a new gravity.

With lives on the line, notions of personal privacy and civil liberty eroded by the heartbeat in countries around the world, regardless of how entrenched, hard-won, or born out of some painful past those notions are. Turbulence in the twentieth century left Europe leery of authoritarian power—especially France, whose principles rose from earlier revolution. In the beginning, France's interior minister, Christophe Castaner, dismissed digital tracking as incompatible with "French culture," citing "individual liberties," the *New York Times* wrote. But no more than three weeks and a tenfold surge in deaths later—an official count of eighteen thousand—President Emmanuel Macron said his government was contemplating a smartphone tracking app based on Singapore's. In the beginning, many criticized China for what they viewed as its draconian telecommunications tracking and movement restrictions. "It's not a good thing," James Hodge, director of the Center for Public Health Law and Policy at Arizona State University, told the CBC, calling China's mass quarantines "a fundamental human-rights violation." Hodge was speaking just one day after the Wuhan quarantine. "That's what's patently unconstitutional." It would not have been possible in the United States or Canada, he said. But a month later, elsewhere in the West, they did exactly that. Beginning with eleven municipalities in northern Italy, police cars blocked roads in and out of the regions and erected barriers. Two weeks after that, Italy—where the term "quarantine" was coined to describe isolation measures during the fourteenth-century Black Death —became the first country to have a nationwide lockdown. Much of the world would follow suit. And people in many countries, for the most part, were surprisingly okay with it.

When I left China, at the Beijing airport, travellers had to complete health declaration cards to leave the country, answering questions such as whether you'd been to Wuhan, where your address was in China, and whether you had been showing any symptoms. A QR-matrix code was plastered at the boarding gate for people to scan with their WeChat Chinese messaging app to aid in contact-tracing. Those measures seemed insignificant at first, barely registering to the mind. But they represented the beginning of something. The idea of the personal liberties Minister Castaner cited, a linchpin of the Western world, would lose ground to collectivism and individual sacrifice for the greater group.

There would also be a shift of a different kind, one harder to describe, yet one felt on a primal level. There would be events that, while not necessarily consequential to society in any big way, were just downright startling. The Netherlands' health minister, strained by his work, would collapse in parliament. A state finance minister from Germany would see the virus situation as hopelessly bleak and kill himself. A German zoo, starved of funding due to the virus, announced it might have to start feeding some of its animals to other animals. The last to die would be a prized, twelve-foot-tall polar bear, the pale beast Vitus. In the United States, eventual meat plant closures forced one farmer to shoot his pigs and send them to the compost. In Israel, wild dogs started prowling the parks from which humans had shied away. It's hard not to see these things as symbols of some sort. I'm sure those looking for it will find a metaphor there—amid the plague, our shepherds break; among baser creation, neighbour might eat neighbour, and the cloven-hooved carcasses pile and rot; and jackals descend upon the Levant.

Later, while reading about the pandemic, out of the corner of my eye, I would chance upon a quote from Russia, about mortality and destiny. We've come to the point that we're quoting those gloomy Eastern writers from the nineteenth century, I thought. Was that Lermontov? Or Gogol? Has to be Chekhov, right? No. It was the modern Russian information official. "Those meant to die will die," he said on television. "Everyone dies."

In a few short weeks, everything would change. A seriousness would descend quickly upon the world. It was as if you were hanging around with pals, beer in hand, telling some off-colour joke, and then Henry Kissinger walked into the room.

On my flight to Singapore, travellers were given their food in boxes instead of trays. Everything they touched was to be thrown away and not used again, just like in the Air China lounge. Even as I left the land, there was a reminder of its virulent sickness that dogged me. I kept my Honeywell H910V mask on for the whole flight.

At the same time, I tried not to think about it. I looked forward to being in Singapore, which was decidedly not Beijing. At the time, outside China, the world had under three hundred cases and just one death. Despite being smack dab in the middle of Asia, Singapore, population 5.6 million, had some thirty infected and no dead. There wasn't much of a virus consciousness in society there. Life was as it would be during any other time. I looked forward to the friends I would see, the fun I would have, the normalcy that I would finally enjoy after two weeks of lockdown.

In leaving Beijing, my dementia-ridden grandfather was also very much on my mind. I wondered what he would make of everything going on around him. He has seen a lot in his lifetime. In China's post-Mao economic reform, he saw his city's metropolitan area quadruple in population to 4 million. Shijiazhuang gained both a subway and an airport in the last decades. My grandparents' previous five-storey, elevator-less apartment building, whose plumbing could not handle toilet paper, was built a year after Mao died. It had been torn down and replaced with a towering condominium whose lift automatically punches in your floor when you swipe your key fob. It was already an unrecognizable world for my grandfather, and in just a few days, it would change again in no less great a magnitude.

I wondered if I would ever see him again, and if I did, how much of my yeye would remain. As disorienting as everything was for me, it must be so much worse for him — the confusion, the fear, the loneliness — assuming he could process such emotions. I thought back to when I got kicked out of the residence, when I sat on a stool on that green spongy floor and held my grandfather's hand. I don't know how much he understood at that moment, but that day, as I was letting go, he held on with all the strength he could muster.

PART TWO
ANATOMY OF A CRISIS

5

Singapore's main airport has duty-free stores for arriving passengers *after* they clear immigration. If you did not buy tax-free booze before your flight, you have another chance when landing. I know about fifty other countries whose airports also have this, including China, but I've somehow never noticed it outside of Singapore. To me, arrival duty-free has always been uniquely Singaporean, speaking to two interrelated perceptions of the country: 1) it is run like a company, ruthlessly efficient and prioritizing profit, and 2) it taxes alcohol ridiculously. If you skip Singapore's arrival duty-free, there will literally be a price to pay. According to one survey, a typical beer at a bar costs $13.47 in Singapore, nearly 50 per cent more than in Beijing—and that survey was done in 2013. However, when I landed at the airport, it was not beer I had in mind as I made directly for the dizzying array of fine single-malt whiskies, which I make a habit of only buying duty-free because of the price and value.

Browsing the shelves, I took off the face mask I wore on the plane. The store was full of passengers arriving from everywhere, from Europe and Africa and Kyrgyzstan, and only a handful of people, notably from the China flights, were wearing masks. Far from the epicentre, I reverted to my pre-China mentality and kept mine off. That turned out to be a bad decision. When I greeted my parents after checking out of the duty-free store, they took a picture with me and posted it to the family WeChat group. My aunt quickly berated me for my bald-faced audacity.

Still reeling from the shame, I walked with my parents to the airport's multi-storey carpark and was instantly slammed by a wall of jarring heat. Singapore's airport is heavily air-conditioned, making the difference between inside and outside all the more apparent. This is a country so close to the equator that there are no seasons and the timings of both sunrise and sunset are nearly constant throughout the year. Every time I go to Singapore—and I've been a lot—I am jolted by the swelter, particularly this time. I boarded my flight amid snow and hail and emerged in a furnace.

Settled at my parents' place, one of the first things I did in Singapore was go for dinner with my friend Kevin, his girlfriend C.J., and some of their quite-well-off friends, who all worked in aviation or finance or aviation finance. Or something like that. I didn't really know any of them, but I'm always up for meeting new people, and anyway, I had been virtually starved of company back in China. One of Kevin's friends, Drew, lived right downtown and had organized pre-drinks at his place. In Singapore, a pad in a location like his can easily cost $2 million. It's likely that Drew did not own it, and his company had simply rented it for him, but still.

I went for drinks with Kevin first, one-on-one, at a craft beer pub with haphazardly strewn furniture, Christmas-esque lights, and a barmaid who seemed too old for her braces. It was in an area called Telok Ayer, which was full of colonial shophouses from back when Singapore was still under British rule. Friday to Sunday nights, some streets are closed to cars, and all the drunken revelry literally pours out onto the road. The area is an interesting mix of beige, short little houses butting right up to the harsh grey and stony towers of banks, law and investment firms, and fancy condominiums like Drew's.

But the contrast is only superficial. The same people work in one area and drink in the other. Beneath all the buildings' facades, beaten daily by the same unforgiving sun, flowed the same money. One of those shophouses, three storeys at most and with little floor space, could easily sell for $10 million.

After each spending $30 on two beers, Kevin and I met C.J. outside her downtown office before going to Drew's apartment, where we would move on from beer to harder liquor and spicy peanuts. I hadn't seen C.J. in person since my internship days eight years ago. Bespectacled and thin — just like Kevin, actually — she looked exactly the same as when I saw her last. The one difference was she wore a face mask.

C.J. was taking the virus a lot more seriously than anyone else in our party of seven that day, and, in retrospect, for good reason.

On the surface, Singapore's tens of cases back then really didn't seem like anything to worry about. But at that point, that was the highest figure outside China, if the *Diamond Princess* cruise ship, anchored off the Port of Yokohama with what was then sixty-one cases, was not included in the count for Japan. Singapore's prime minister, Lee Hsien Loong, told his country that many of its cases did not appear to have been brought in from the outside. "We've seen some cases which cannot be traced to the source of infection," he said in televised remarks. The virus was likely already spreading locally within Singapore, instances of transmission between those who had never even been to China. "These worried us," Lee said.

It was barely two weeks after the epicentre of Wuhan had been sealed off. It didn't take a lot or long for the virus to journey some three thousand kilometres south to Singapore, crossing borders and the South China Sea. But then again, such things never do. Even just two weeks earlier, when I'd landed in Beijing, two days before the Year of the Rat began, COVID-19 had fanned out with a ferocity that nobody at the time knew. As later investigations would suggest, far across the Pacific Ocean, within California's Bay Area community, the virus was already spreading.

COVID-19 is not the first of its kind. In make-up, it is much like SARS (severe acute respiratory syndrome), of the early 2000s, or MERS (Middle East respiratory syndrome), of 2012. They all belong to the family of coronaviruses, named with the Latin word for crown because their shape under a microscope looks like one. They spread through the air in droplets produced when an infected person coughed or sneezed, or through contaminated surfaces. The first so-called super-spreader of SARS, a fishmonger in southern China, infected thirty nurses and doctors when he went to the hospital. Within a month after that, SARS had spread as far as Canada, when a woman brought it to

Toronto from Hong Kong. She infected her son, who then brought the virus to the local hospital, resulting in an unprecedented World Health Organization warning for the city. I remember those days in Singapore, when schools were suspended and suspected carriers quarantined.

While similar, though, COVID-19 is also different. Neither SARS's nor MERS's death toll even pierced the four digits. Among them, COVID-19 is the lone disease classified as a pandemic, an epidemic that has spread across a large region — multiple continents or worldwide, for example — affecting a large population, and whose numbers have not been stabilized. This new coronavirus was worse than what had come before. One of the reasons for this, ironically, is that COVID-19 is less deadly and debilitating.

The symptoms, such as breathing difficulties, are more severe for SARS, so the infected are rushed to the hospital and treated. Or they die. About 10 per cent of SARS patients die, whereas only some 3 per cent of COVID-19 carriers do. And dead and hospitalized people generally do not go out into the community to spread the disease, wittingly or not. With COVID-19, on the other hand, most do not require hospitalization, and sometimes the symptoms do not even present. You go about daily life, passing it to others, who pass it to even more others, possibly never knowing that you ever had it. "That's why 'nightmare' viruses — like those with 90 per cent mortality — thankfully aren't always very successful," Dr. Zania Stamataki, a lecturer in viral immunology, wrote in the *Guardian*. "To survive and thrive, a virus must operate like a spy in enemy territory, skilled at passing its genetic material." While it took eighty days for the United States to get to 500,000 cases, it took just eighteen days to double that to a million. Because of how mild it is, COVID-19 spreads more quickly and widely, so much so that even though the percentage of infected people it kills is small, the sheer numbers are staggering, and along with them, the panic and fear they cause.

Among the most dreadful projections was one by Imperial College London, which predicted a worst-case scenario of 510,000 deaths in the United Kingdom and 2.2 million in the United States. That model assumed no physical-distancing measures, however, so it is highly unlikely the numbers will escalate to that level. Other estimates for U.S. deaths have ranged between 71,000 and 1.7 million. But the thing with such wildly varying forecasts—and not to mention the rapidly changing situation—is most will turn out inaccurate. The main projection model put out by the United States government initially put deaths at reaching 60,000 only in August 2020. It passed that figure in April. The truth is, we can't really know the scale of it. Even official counts are often too low. In the United Kingdom, the *Financial Times* estimated actual deaths to be more than double the figure given by the authorities, what with some people dying in their homes or without being tested. In Indonesia, according to a *Reuters* analysis, it could be nearly triple. Some hospitals ran out of body bags. And even though people do die all the time, and a couple of million may not seem to some to be significant for a planet of billions, the COVID-19-era dead are not people who would have died anyway. The *New York Times* calculated its city's mortality rates during one month of the crisis. It found the figure to be more than twice the usual number of deaths during the same period in previous years, far outstripping even the month of the 9/11 extremist attack—and still, that might not be the full tally. "Even this is only a partial count; we expect this number to rise as more deaths are counted," the *Times* wrote.

There are the indirect impacts. The U.S. Centers for Disease Control and Prevention's projections suggest 2.4 million to 21 million of the infected could require hospitalization—internal figures leaked to media—but the country has under 1 million staffed hospital beds. People with non-COVID-19 ailments face a stretched healthcare system. They might even avoid hospitals or the doctor's office because of the fear of being infected. A cardiologist told the *Times* he was particularly concerned about patients with heart conditions—"that the overall toll is much greater." It is in fact impossible to tell how great the total deaths will be. German chancellor Angela Merkel notably said up to 70 per cent of her citizens would end up getting infected by COVID-19. The Czech Republic's prime minister accused her of causing panic. But Merkel's was a view backed by experts, and it opened the floodgates for other politicians to speak the same unpleasant truth.

Robert A. Jensen, the chairman of Kenyon International, a firm that helps communities respond to crises, told the *Times* the virus would leave a lasting mark. "The reminders will be cemeteries," he said, describing European burial plots for the 1918 Spanish flu pandemic, which actually had little to do with Spain but killed 50 million people according to some estimates. Today's graveyards, similarly, will have entire sections devoted to deaths during the pandemic, Jensen said. This comparison of COVID-19 to the Spanish flu pandemic was most poignant. While it is hard to find parallels for the coronavirus outbreak, with respect to the impact on the world, older pandemics come close, sometimes eerily so.

There is something about COVID-19 that evokes history. The media is flush with such comparisons, particularly to an event even older than the Spanish flu: the bubonic plague, which has existed since the Bronze Age. The iteration that marked the fourteenth century, dubbed the Black Death, has been the most famous, wiping out upward of 200 million people and half of Europe. That was the beginning of the second plague pandemic. It took two hundred years for population levels to get back to where they were when the Black Death started, by which time another major outbreak loomed, as the pestilence repeatedly returned to haunt Europe and the Mediterranean. The great minds that feature heavily in Western education, taught and retaught in schools, such as Isaac Newton and William Shakespeare, were themselves shaped by the plague, producing some of their best work under the resulting disruption. In Europe and the Middle East, the plague has "occupied a central place in the collective memories of those populations for the last six centuries," as the historian Suzanne Austin Alchon writes in *A Pest in the Land*. The Black Death has been the stuff of literature, entire museum sections, and popular culture, and even seared into the minds of schoolchildren.

Comparing something like COVID-19 to plagues of the past is a natural and even useful thing to do, at least on some levels, but we should be careful in taking it too far, at least for the time being. For one thing, based on the present numbers, COVID-19 hasn't killed nearly as many people. Biologically, it is fundamentally different from the bubonic plague. The current pandemic exists in a far more developed world. For example, during the Black Death, neither indoor plumbing nor the concept of washing hands had been invented. Medicine was only in its infancy at the time. But the similarities are sometimes uncanny, as observers of all sorts noted: European ports quarantined passengers from incoming ships. On land, during the second plague pandemic, cities formed "sanitary cordons" that restricted movement. Within their walls, health authorities hauled off plague victims for isolation. People were prevented from selling clothes. Public gatherings were banned. In France, an official would go to every house and lock the doors like a jail warden. Describing the Italian city-state Naples during the plague, the scholar Frank Snowden writes in *Epidemics and Society*, "Every activity of normal life ceased amidst shuttered shops, unemployment and hunger." Rumours spread of malicious actors purposely spreading the plague, and across Europe, people blamed perceived outsiders such as the Jewish community. In the present crisis, now that Europe had had the world's biggest COVID-19 outbreaks, all the current misinformation and fresh hostility toward Asians evokes vividly that shameful episode of continental history.

And such evocations can go back even further, to the first bubonic pandemic, the Plague of Justinian in the sixth century. The economy and public spaces were decimated, and confinement and isolation ran rampant in society. Now, amid the COVID-19 pandemic, Jordina Sales Carbonell, a researcher at the University of Barcelona, wrote that, 1,500 years ago, "certain similarities and parallels observed in human behavior with regard to a virus and its consequences seem so familiar and contemporary."

———

Back in Singapore, after pre-drinks at Drew's apartment, our party of seven had dinner at a Japanese restaurant by the river. It was close to downtown, but far enough that we had to divide ourselves into two hired cars, a most harrowing journey for Kevin, Drew, and two others. Whoever booked the car had typed the wrong address into the app, and that group unwittingly ended up at the restaurant's corporate headquarters. It was about half an hour before they made it back to the correct place. Sacrifice is sometimes needed for the greater food.

Drew had specifically picked out the restaurant, which specialized in a sort of Japanese savoury pancake called *okonomiyaki*. The restaurant had a rather cozy, at-home atmosphere — dimly lit, with shelves of manga comic books lining the walls. The restaurant was so notable, it had been featured on television in Japan. It was almost always fully booked, and that day, even as threats of contagion loomed, it was no exception. Of course, the virus was still never far from the conversation that night.

Everyone at our dinner was some sort of exile from Hong Kong or mainland China, waiting out the worst in what was thought to be a safer place. While the tropical city-state technically had more virus cases, Hong Kong is right next to the mainland and had not restricted travel from there on a similar level. The territory was thus deemed as bad as mainland China, an extension of it — due not so much to the virus itself but to the social and societal disruption caused by it. I was in a different situation from the others, but there was a fundamental similarity: I was supposed to be in Hong Kong, but I was not. It didn't feel like it at the time, but looking back, ahead of what is possibly the biggest crisis of our generation, we were already fleeing the infected areas.

Eventually, the world would see a greater version of what could be called the flight of the rich play out in New York, which later became a major outbreak centre. Analyzing smartphone location data, the *New York Times* would find that populations in the city's wealthiest neighbourhoods decreased by nearly half during the pandemic. Altogether, nearly half a million people would flee New York. The hardest hit in the city would be the poor, exactly as they were during the plague seven centuries ago.

The comparison of COVID-19 to historical pandemics isn't so much in the specific traits of the pathogens or how we are equipped to handle them—or even the death toll. "The most disturbing similarity . . . lies not in the diseases themselves but in their social consequences," wrote a doctoral candidate at Durham University. It's the widespread disruption caused, the realization that the world we have come to know has become foreign. In recent memory, in addition to SARS and MERS, we've weathered AIDS; the H1N1 virus, with different strains called swine or bird flu; and Ebola. But the scale of the disruption to daily life brought by COVID-19 dwarfs them all. As the Barcelonan researcher Sales Carbonell wrote about the Plague of Justinian, "despite the tragedy we are all personally experiencing, it remains a source of wonderment how history repeats."

If that is so, though, if we can see our current situation so clearly in our past, then we can see our future, too, in how those historical events resolved. The natural inference is that all the changes to our existence now are only the beginning. After all, the bubonic plague did not just change the face of society at the time of its outbreaks. It also shaped its future.

6

The long-prevailing system in medieval Europe, after the fall of the Roman Empire, was that the king owned all land, which he partitioned to aristocrats, who in turn had serfs who did the farming and paid a portion of the proceeds to the crown. The serfs were quasi-slaves who, themselves, typically earned nothing. Europe was also severely over-populated at the time, *Ancient History Encyclopedia* writes, a condition that upheld the status quo; there was no shortage of serfs, who had little bargaining power because they were so easily replaceable. Such was life, plowing the land from the time they could until they collapsed, a life lived with a bowed head. Then their children did the same. But when the Black Death gutted the population, labour became a valuable commodity. The smallfolk started dressing and eating better. They started forgetting their place. Three major uprisings of the lower classes broke out between 1358 and 1381, and it wasn't long before serfdom became rare in Western Europe. The better lives that most eventually enjoyed—the greater longevity and the upheaval of the long-standing socio-economic order—were a direct consequence of the plague. Cardinal Francis Aidan Gasquet, a twentieth-century British historical scholar, writes that the plague had created, for the first time, a middle class.

There was also an upheaval of the mind. In the Black Death's aftermath, "doctors," who had thought the plague spread by bad air or "miasma," and who had come up with no cure, came under scrutiny. So did the clergy, which had previously so dominated society, for all the charms and amulets, religious gatherings, prayer, and fasting did nothing to ward off the plague, *Ancient History Encyclopedia* writes. Whatever god or gods people prayed to were dwarfed by the one whose name was Death, who gave no preferential treatment to friars, monks, nuns, or priests. Yet, such a close brush with mortality, such trauma, also led to extreme outpourings of religious piety from some survivors. Suffice to say, the result of the Black Death was a great increase in critical thinking and introspection in society. There are some who even say that it was this shift that heralded the Renaissance that began in Italy, a period of rapid development in art, architecture, politics, science, and literature in Europe. This is often challenged, of course. Such historical causes can only be attributed hundreds of years later, and there is often little definitive way to prove theories right or wrong. Nothing ever has just one factor. But what is undisputed is the timing. The Black Death marked a turning point.

Such is the power of a great plague, typhoid supposedly smoothed the conquering path of certain conquistadors. Measles or smallpox is said to have contributed to the fall of the Roman Empire. The bubonic plague was speculated to have done the same to its successor, the Byzantine Empire. Infectious diseases throughout history, scholars, media, and historians say, have crushed revolutions, sparked socio-economic reform, tipped the scales of wars, and reshaped how entire countries viewed religion. Beyond their death tolls, every plague has left a lasting legacy. We live in a world defined by past pandemics. From a longer-term perspective, the repaving of the path of Europe is actually the least of the effects of the second plague pandemic that started with the Black Death.

One of the reasons COVID-19 is so evocative of that ancient pestilence is, perhaps, that many of the containment measures we've seen during the present crisis were developed back then. Quarantine came from the term *quaranta giorni*, Italian for forty days, the period visitors to Venetian ports needed to be isolated. Across Europe, the segregation of the infected; the locking of people in their homes in plague-ridden towns; the monitoring of people's health and their registration in a central database; even the regulation of butcher meat—all these were done back then, in a widespread and systematic manner, largely for the first time. The authority given to enforce these measures was the first form of an institutionalized public healthcare, the scholar Frank Snowden writes. And that had much wider implications.

Beyond taxation, medieval governments had had little direct role in their citizens' lives. But with the plague, what began as temporary health agencies eventually became permanent, heralding "a vast extension of state power into spheres of human life that had never been subject to political authority," Frank Snowden writes in *Epidemics and Society*. When states started assuming responsibility for the safeguarding of health, they also started to have a greater role in the upholding of borders, in record-keeping, and in the organization, segmentation, and monitoring of their people. According to the philosopher Michel Foucault, the plague-induced rules and restrictions on daily life evolved into systematic power structures, and the close eye kept on people under lockdown gave birth to the concept of government surveillance. With the pestilence, there was a radical expansion in the role governments had in the lives of their people, which endures to this day as the modern state, Snowden told an interviewer: To do more, those in power needed more taxation, more hospitals, more laws, and more people to enforce them. Greater government often begets even greater government.

7

"You just came back from Beijing?" C.J. asked me rather pointedly as we sat at the Japanese restaurant, waiting for Kevin, Drew, and the others to finally arrive after going to the wrong spot. There was an unmistakable worry in her eyes and voice.

I had never hidden that fact. I had been in constant contact with Kevin, and he knew full well where I'd been, so I'd assumed C.J. knew. And I had posted liberally on social media. In the car over to the restaurant, I had mentioned the trip rather casually. Now I was regretting it.

"Shouldn't you be isolating yourself?" she asked. "Nobody said anything to you at the airport?"

Nobody did, in fact. And truth be told, while I did read the news at the time, I hadn't paid attention to any specific travel restrictions or containment measures. All I knew was that, for me, travel went on largely as normal. Still, C.J. was clearly uncomfortable, and that made me uncomfortable.

"Do you want me to leave?" I asked.

When the rest arrived, we switched topics. The matter wasn't brought up again, even as, sometimes, we still talked about the virus itself. That night, C.J.'s concerns were never far from my mind.

Turns out, it wasn't just my mind this thought weighed on but pretty much the whole population of Singapore. As the number of cases there grew, instant noodles, rice, and toilet paper started flying off the shelves as residents stockpiled in a frenzy. More and more, the masks went on.

One day, I was at a supermarket with my mother. All I wanted was a pack of potato chips. There had been a craze in recent years for hipsterish, hyperlocal flavours based on national dishes such as chicken rice, whose fragrant grains are made in a special blend of poultry broth and garlic; *laksa*, seafood noodles in a spicy, creamy base made with coconut milk; and *nasi lemak*, rice made with coconut milk as well, and served with fried chicken and sweet chilli. Another trend in snacks had been fried fish skin coated with salted egg yolk, which tastes like a better version of potato chips. My mouth had been watering just thinking of those. But when we saw the queues that formed long into the empty aisles, my mother and I decided to just go home.

The stockpiling we had witnessed had something to do with beliefs in the breakdown of supply chains due to increasing travel restrictions, which could theoretically cause food and necessities to become unavailable. It also had something to do with the belief that a potential lockdown would just unilaterally keep everyone indoors, forbidding any venturing outside. News of supply shortages in Hong Kong did not help. Besides being a huge inconvenience, nothing says end-of-days panic like fevered stockpiling.

In a leaked audio clip, it became clear this wasn't lost on Singapore's trade and industry minister, Chan Chun Sing, who looked like he cut his own hair, even before the eventual COVID-19 lockdowns. He called the stockpilers "idiots" and "disgraceful" in an unusually slang-filled tirade, even for him. In formal settings, Singapore is a land of English, but in day-to-day life, that English is often watered down with loan-phrases from the local Chinese, Malay, and Indian communities. It's a bit like Jamaican patois. Chan's past colloquialisms have been trademark. This time, caught in an unvarnished private moment, Chan was an unprecedented blend of buddy-buddy politician and *beng*, local slang for a ne'er-do-well young man of low education, like a British chav or yob.

The audio clip of Chan was unique for how funny and lowbrow it was. He had always been informal, but never like this. The man had graduated from the University of Cambridge! Chan's tirade stood in stark contrast to the measured, roundabout answers he normally gave when I was a reporter there. This recent twenty-five-minute soliloquy was complete with diarrhea and masturbation jokes and included endearing terms such as *sia suay* ("disgraceful"), *buay tahan* ("cannot endure"), and *wah lau eh* (a catch-all exclamation whose origin is debatable, but which some say is related to male anatomy). What wasn't funny about his tirade was what it symbolized—the image of a breakdown in authority in a place where authority just doesn't break down. How quickly, I thought, it can all go to pieces.

Despite Minister Chan's profanity-laden stand-up routine and the shell-shocked shoppers I saw, grabbing instant noodles like Incan gold, the eventual lockdowns hadn't yet descended. The life that I had in Singapore in February would become nearly unfathomable in a month's time; I had some sort of social engagement almost every day I was there. I was at pubs. I was at restaurants. I was on public transit all the time. I went axe-throwing. I went to a professional wrestling match for the first time. My friends and I tried out an escape room, failing miserably. I went rock climbing three times a week. I even went to Malaysia, twice—a time-honoured national pastime for people in Singapore, no more than an hour away from the peninsula from any part of the island.

Such travel is a popular Singaporean activity mostly for financial reasons, and its origin goes back decades. Sometime after the Second World War, with the British Empire fading, the former colonies Malaysia and Singapore became one country. Then, Singapore became, to my knowledge, the lone nation in the history of the entire world to gain independence involuntarily. Malaysia kicked it out. Singapore's leader at the time, the country's first prime minister, was Lee Kuan Yew, father of Lee Hsien Loong, who later became the third prime minister. Back then, Lee the elder had cried on television at the separation, and it was all a very big deal. But it turned out to be a blessing, as Lee, by many metrics, managed Singapore well. What was once a one-to-one exchange between the Singapore dollar and Malaysian ringgit became almost one-to-three. At one point, so many Singaporeans were crossing the border for lower-priced petrol, the country forced every car going into Malaysia to have at least three-quarters of a full tank. Everything in Malaysia was significantly cheaper. One of its slogans had been, "Malaysia Boleh!" which had been interpreted by Singaporeans as "anything goes in Malaysia." There, among certain young men, various places of ill-repute are, in fact, especially reputable. Nicotine vaporizers, illegal in one country, are plentiful in the other. Fine dining can be had for the price of takeout. Whatever your taste, many different sorts of entertainment can be found for a reasonable price just an hour away.

On my first trip to Malaysia, though, I would find that while life can sometimes be hard, it is always harder when you have no luck. I got stuck at the border.

Going before immigration, I had to be separated for extra health screening because I had recently been to China. Young men in light-blue protective gear made me fill out a form and repeatedly took my temperature.

"Where in China did you go?" asked one of them.

"Beijing," I said. In that general area, at least. Adding Shijiazhuang to my answer, I figured, would lead only to confusion.

But apparently, Beijing was confusion enough. The protective-gear-clad staff pored over a chart on the wall in their cramped office to see if Beijing was among the list of cities that they needed to worry about.

While they did that, a guy with a buzz cut and broad face, who somehow looked both slithery and rodent-like at the same time, laughed at me, saying, "Quarantine, quarantine." He knew only two English words, both of which were the same. And then, like that, I was on my way. They must have found China's capital on a map, determined it wasn't under quarantine, and decided I wasn't a threat.

Later, in a car from a ride-hailing service, I heard the driver complain the city was slowly sinking into a mini-recession. The major Malaysian city near the border, Johor Bahru, is sustained almost exclusively by tourists coming from the Singaporean side. With the decline in travel due to the virus, everyone was making less money.

On the second trip to Malaysia, a friend and I went to Legoland. If you wonder what business two grown men could have in what is essentially a children's theme park, then you did not grow up obsessed with Lego like I did. I had been dreaming of going to the theme park ever since it opened. Yet on the day of our visit, the park was nearly empty. Only one of its restaurants was open, and its efforts to make fries into the shape of Lego bricks was sorely disappointing. I don't know if it was because of the virus or because the theme park was just in decline, but it was depressing nonetheless.

The wrestling matches we went to, in the centre of Singapore's bar and clubbing district, had something of a COVID-19 theme. The villainous character, the Coloniser—a blond, powerfully built Caucasian woman dressed all in white, and who sometimes had an Asian manservant as part of her act—had widely disparaged Singaporean culture while purposely mispronouncing the names of local food, such as *roti prata*, a type of savoury Indian pancake, usually served with curry. Evoking the country's past British overlords, the Coloniser then made racist remarks about the virus while spraying the air around her with disinfectant. In the world of staged wrestling, she's called a "heel," someone the audience is supposed to root against. The Coloniser—in real life, as it turns out, a doctorate holder born and bred in Singapore—was obvious to the point of beating the message in with a stick. There was immense laughter from the crowd, which chanted, "Wuhan! Wuhan!" in response, expressing solidarity with the infected against the wrestler, in a deliberately ironic manner. I can't remember if the Coloniser won or lost, but days later, when I wasn't three beers in, I found the virus bit a lot less funny.

Then came a text message from C.J.

"I spoke with my dad and a cousin who works in a hospital, and their advice is to quarantine yourself for 10–14 days if you just arrived from China," she said. "There will always be some risk and everyone needs to be responsible in taking care of their own hygiene.

"You don't have to follow this advice, but these are scary times and frankly I do not want the risk of bringing this infection to my elderly relatives."

At the time, I brushed off her concern. I did not even know C.J. that well. My primary connection had been with Kevin. But my ties with Kevin are important to me, and I did not want to put him in a difficult position. They lived with each other, after all.

Kevin had texted me after C.J.'s message: "Sorry if C.J. messaged you anything about quarantining yourself. She was freaking out a bit because I think she's anxious about her family and older relatives."

"Hey no worries. It's all good," I responded. "I guess if you're still here next Friday we can go for another drink . . . then it will be two weeks after I'm back—considering C.J.'s concerns."

I wasn't sure what to say to C.J., though. It was one of those situations in which someone explains something technical, and you might respond, "I see," but you don't really see, and I didn't want to just say, "I see," because it sounds curt. I thus never responded to her.

The fact was, though, that Singapore, which had started reporting daily infection numbers and death tolls, was becoming exactly what

I'd hoped it wouldn't. Over the sunny little island, a dark silhouette grew by the day.

Anticipating gradually worse travel conditions all over the world, I decided to make some changes to my onward journey from Singapore. I had what can only be described as a special ticket, purchased with airline miles. I was able to game the system to get a complicated, multi-city itinerary that would normally cost tens of thousands of dollars for just the price of a round-trip ticket. I could have up to sixteen stops, anywhere in the world, and I had intended to make full use of it. Ultimately planning to end up in Germany, I had added in a slew of stopovers drawn from my love for both history and off-beat travel. There were ancient cities such as Istanbul, Cairo, and Athens, and the capitals of the post-9/11 wars, Kabul and Baghdad. The latter two destinations are not places I would normally think of going, but adding them to my trip had been effectively free, so I thought, why not? However, with the virus situation becoming worse every day, my original itinerary did not seem like a great idea. Moreover, the United States had just assassinated an Iranian general in Iraq. Breakfast in Baghdad did not sound nearly as attractive as it had before. I decided to bypass all of those cities and just go straight to Germany.

My choices and experience must have been relatable because the whole world seemed to have the exact same idea of changing their tickets at precisely the same time. Because of COVID-19 and its travel disruptions, the mileage-program call-in lines were jammed in a way that I had never before experienced. Even getting on a waitlist was fortunate. Sometimes the lines were so full, I couldn't even be placed on hold. Due to the special nature of my ticket, the only way to change it was by phone. I was on hold for more than two hours, and when I got through to change it, the operator herself had to be put on hold by someone else within her organization. Then my call was dropped at the moment when my old ticket had been cancelled but my new one had yet to be booked. It was as if I had managed to walk between rain-drops. I was on hold for another two hours and then had to explain everything to a completely different operator who, God bless her, took only another hour to navigate the mayhem and change my ticket accordingly. And the call centre was only staffed during office hours in North America. I was up all night.

Near the end of my stay in Singapore, it started feeling like whatever bubble I had been living in had burst. It wasn't that anything of great consequence had happened to me, but there were warning shots, hints that wherever I travelled to, COVID-19 would rear its ugly head. There was no safe zone.

I had had the great pleasure of having no cellphone reception almost the entire time I was in Singapore; my Canadian telecommunications company had removed the Asian city-state from the list of places to which it provides roaming. I was more than fine with this, for most of my important communications are done through email or instant messag-ing such as WhatsApp, and I rarely have people with serious matters calling me unscheduled. Those calls I did need to make, like the ones changing my travel itinerary, were made on my parents' phone. But at some point, while I was lunching at a country club with my father, it became clear that Singapore had miraculously been added back to my telco's roaming list. For a while, as we sat at the club by the water, just across the straits from Malaysia, the sun dull upon the surface, my phone started to vibrate uncontrollably. It had never done that before. The real world was coming for me, a little earlier than I wanted or expected.

Increasingly, I saw hints of the pandemic in my own life. A friend of mine in Singapore is originally from Wuhan. He had two relatives infected, one of whom had died. His parents—allegedly members of the Communist Party, according to other friends—had gotten out of Wuhan just before the lockdown, leading some to question whether they'd acted on prior knowledge. His parents ended up quarantined in Singapore. Another friend, an American living in Singapore with his family, still in university, had to tell his father he was out studying to hang out with the rest of our group of friends. He had been banned from all nonessential interactions.

My father is an engineer for a company that makes pharmaceutical equipment. The wife of one of my father's colleagues was suspected of becoming infected, and the entire office started working from home. She ended up cleared, but the work structure did not go back to normal. Eventually, major companies in Singapore, such as banks and commercial research laboratories, redistributed their workers into team-siloes at different locations, so that if one group goes down for some reason, the organization continues to function. My father's company and those of many of my friends adopted this model. That siloing extended even to non-work interactions. When my father made plans for a social meetup with a work friend, the primary consideration was: "We're from the same silo. I guess it should be okay."

I haven't lived with my parents for nearly a decade. On that trip to Singapore, I noticed they had developed a curious new ritual, at least curious for them. Every day, after dinner, they sat together on the sofa to watch the news. I found it a heartening thing for my parents to do, who are approaching their sixties and seem to have grown a lot closer since I and my younger sister both left the nest. Their newfound attention to the news also suggested a sort of respect for the journalism that is my profession, I felt.

"When did you start doing that?" I asked.

"Oh, we've never done it until now," my mother responded. "It's only because of the virus."

Along with the daily tallies of infection rates and deaths, every now and then, Prime Minister Lee Hsien Loong—popular, but increasingly frail-looking after stumbling on live television in 2016—would address the nation. My parents watched with an eagle-eyed intensity that was sort of unnerving.

Despite the circumstances, I was happy to have spent time with them. It was hard to say when I'd see them next given the growing travel restrictions and the quickly collapsing state of affairs in general, but we were good at staying in touch and keeping up to date. My main concern in departing was what I would encounter next. Thus far, the virus had followed me like a shadow. I had watched in real time as China and now Singapore strained under the weight—the fear it engendered and the prospect of the unknown looming everywhere. Needless to say, this wasn't the trip I had planned or hoped for. As I prepared to head to Germany, for most of the world, this month of March was to be a rude introduction to something already changing everything we knew.

PART THREE
RIPPLES ACROSS THE POND

8

On the plane to Germany, Turkish Airlines handed out contact-tracing forms for COVID-19. Despite cutting out all the stops between Singapore and Germany, I couldn't get a direct flight and had to transfer in Istanbul. I was going to pass through what was formerly Constantinople regardless, through the city famously devastated by the sixth-century Plague of Justinian. And the Turkish government needed to know the contact details of everyone, no matter how brief their stay in the country, so if someone ended up with the virus, officials could track how it spread. I dutifully filled mine out and handed it in.

After a short layover in Istanbul, I slept through most of the flight to Munich, during which I had an aisle seat. A German woman beside me, next to the window, would climb over me to use the washroom, her shoeless feet on the armrests, to avoid waking me. This did wake me up, but I appreciated the gesture nonetheless, and was kind of impressed at her agility. With the eventual decline in air travel and physical distancing measures making passengers sit farther apart, that dexterous dance would become a thing of the past—and fast. But that did not occur to me then.

At the time of my travel, Germany had a zero mortality rate, and was still holding soccer matches with tens of thousands of spectators. In France, which had only a handful of deaths, President Emmanuel Macron and his wife attended the theatre. Nearly a hundred countries were now reporting cases of COVID-19, but air travel was still relatively the same as when I'd flown to Beijing. The West still hadn't taken the matter seriously. Amid the bustle of everyday life, few heard the low hum of the looming menace.

Germany was where I had spent ages one through six. I had a lot of people to see in the country, although most were those I met later in life, elsewhere. The fact that I had cut out all the stops between Singapore and Germany, however, all the cities from Kabul to Athens, meant I ended up in Germany much earlier than planned. So, I settled in the empty apartment of my close friend Elias. Elias is Canadian, a dual citizen of Finland, and was pursuing a master's degree in Germany. When I arrived, Elias was in Canada seeing friends and family. I had originally planned to meet him in Germany only at the tail end of my month-long trip to Europe.

I collected Elias's apartment key from his friend Risako, a Japanese exchange student studying Germanic literature, who says she reads one German novel a week. We met at the train station and walked toward the apartment, my wheeled suitcase bouncing up and down the cobblestones. Risako gave me some pierogi and waffles, saying that because the next day was Sunday, no shops would be open. It was the law, and the Germans were particularly strict about such things. There was a genuineness to Risako, a kindness that was more than politeness. Her life's purpose, her raison d'être — or the Japanese version, *ikigai*, as I like to think — is to bring happiness to others, she said. I took an instant liking to Risako, despite a bit of a language barrier. We did have two common tongues, but English was her worst language, and German mine.

Elias lived in Bayreuth, in the state of Bavaria, two hours north of Munich, where I had landed. It was a small town of 75,000 people where the composer Richard Wagner had built his opera house, financed by his eccentric patron, King Ludwig II. Bayreuth had also been a centre of Nazi ideology, what with Adolf Hitler being a huge Wagner fan. Sixty kilometres away, as the raven flies, was Nuremberg, where the courtroom for post–Second World War trials was still in use by the local judiciary.

While Risako and I struck up a friendship, there in Bayreuth, in the last days of winter, everything in Europe started to change. It began in the south, across the snow-dusted Alps. "Italians woke up on Sunday morning, and it was already the future," one journalist astutely wrote at the time: Haphazardly and suddenly, Rome placed heavy movement restrictions across the wealthy north, corralling 16 million people and more or less locking them in place. Vatican sermons had to come via video from the book room. "This Pope is caged in the library," the pontiff Francis said. Eventually, the whole of the country was locked down as Italy's death toll neared the world's highest and parts of its healthcare system, as one administrator told media, ended up "on the brink of collapse." Other parts of Europe would follow. The Second

World War comparisons started coming, which were apt, for even French cafés that had been open through the Nazi occupation shut their doors.

When I left China in February, even though I had been there, I believed that this was something that would more or less remain contained to those borders. I thought I had escaped the worst of it, the lockdown, social isolation, and the fear that accompanied COVID-19. Even in my time in Singapore, with paranoia mounting, the numbers of infected and dead were low, and I couldn't help thinking that people, like C.J., for example, were overreacting. If anything, being in Singapore solidified my feeling that COVID-19 had not spread much, even in Asia. A concern, for sure, but one linked almost solely to China. Arriving in Germany had seemed like a welcome relief; I was out of Asia, out of reach of the virus and the baggage that came with it. Few protective measures were in place, and the air was calm. Then, in what seemed like an instant, Italy and Spain each reported four-digit growths in new cases, and Europe's infection numbers surged to more than 36,000, growing by nearly 50 per cent. Barring China, the continent would have more cases than the rest of the world combined. The World Health Organization labelled Europe the new epicentre, and global deaths topped 5,000. There was alarm and panic like what I saw in China just a month ago. And it rippled. Global financial markets, already beaten, would suffer wallop after wallop, hearkening back to Great Depression–era plunges. In fact, the International Monetary Fund would warn about the world's worst downturn since then. Even Bitcoin crashed. Everything seemed to be happening at once. In the husk of downtown Bayreuth, I was reliving what I had just left behind, like some terrible version of *Groundhog Day,* wondering how everything had turned so bad so quickly.

I think that at least part of the answer is us. It is Elias and me, born and brought up around the world, speaking many languages, living in many places, splitting time between different countries—we are globalized, perhaps more than any generation that preceded us. Like the plague spreading around trade routes, the coronavirus was moving with the flow of people, aided in great part by cheaper and faster travel, and an economy that sees few borders. In one of the more spectacular displays, a British national picked up the virus in Singapore at a business conference, then went skiing in France before returning home. From one person, eleven ended up hospitalized over three countries. And it is more than increased travel. In the past, a company might design, source, and manufacture all in one spot, but that has become increasingly rare. Now, the webs of supply chains and relationships are increasingly interwoven around the world. That increasing interconnectedness has made the effects of pandemics so much worse. More than shaping the lives of those like me, globalization has defined the entire twenty-first century, and so, like never before, small disturbances can ripple into tidal waves.

9

I grew up in Wuppertal in the 1990s, a city of 350,000 just east of the river Rhine, famous for its *schwebebahn*, a suspended transit system whose rails and wheels are on top. My father was then a graduate student at the local university. We lived at an address on Paulussenstraße, which we rented from Frau Petrick, an avid gardener who was very kind to me once by pretending to be frightened when I ambushed her in a homemade mask. I thoroughly enjoyed my time in Germany, despite sticking out sorely as an ethnic minority. All the local kids thought I was from Japan, and I was too awkward to correct them.

You can't really blame them, though. Back then, it was a little after the Berlin Wall fell, when Japan, despite a recession, was still the world's largest economy after the United States, not that different from China now. It feels funny recounting this, as if talking about events from centuries ago when it was not even thirty years. But a lot can happen in that time. China back then was viewed maybe just a little more charitably than North Korea. Soldiers had opened fire on protestors, and an estimated hundreds to thousands died during the crackdown in

Tiananmen Square. I don't think many Germans at the time imagined they would ever see a person from China in real life. Yet the seeds of change had been planted just a few years earlier by, of all things, the opening in 1987 of the first KFC in Beijing. And with that and what that symbolized, what was once dubbed the "sick man of Asia" was set on a path to overtake Japan as the world's second-largest economy. Key factors in realizing that status were China's ability—through sheer numbers and the centralized power of the ruling Communist Party—to provide cheap labour and manufacturing unmatched in the rest of the world; its increasing cross-border relations; and a proliferation of trade due to rising globalization. Rather quickly, China went from being a poor and agrarian country with relatively few ties outside its borders to being a presence in just about every country in the world. Not long ago, a novel coronavirus that started in China would probably have stayed in China. Indeed, my kneejerk thinking when I left there was that the virus wouldn't follow. I should have known better.

In *The Hitchhiker's Guide to the Galaxy* series, the humourist Douglas Adams writes about how dependent the quintessential human male is on his community: "Left to his own devices he couldn't build a toaster. He could just about make a sandwich and that was it." Someone actually put that theory to the test. "I'm trying to build a toaster, from scratch—beginning by mining the raw materials and ending with a product that . . . sells for only £3.99," the British designer Thomas Thwaites wrote on the website for his book *The Toaster Project*. He failed miserably. Our world has become so interconnected, the web of supply chains so vast and intricate, a simple toaster requires some four hundred components, sourced from all over the globe. The core driver of that was the pursuit of efficiency and better profit margins, accelerated by globalization, and Thwaites was hardly the first to realize that.

In 1958, the American economist Leonard Read wrote an essay titled "I, Pencil." It was from that writing instrument's point of view, detailing the sheer complexity of its creation—such that "not a single person on the face of this earth knows how to make me," the pencil said. That statement applies for a toaster, a pencil, or anything at all for that matter. It exemplifies the extensive divisions of labour that have come to define our economy, distilled into the credo that people should all be doing what they do best. The required cedar for the pencil grows in Northern California and Oregon, whose farmers have made a name for themselves for providing such wood. The resultant logs are shipped to San Leandro, California, to be cut, where the area's millwrights specialize in that, having trained for years and to do it better than their competitors. The graphite is mined in Sri Lanka, then mixed with clay from Mississippi and treated with wax from Mexico, and the oil that goes into the rubber is from Indonesia—all areas where such materials are the most easily obtained. Stretching supply lines around the world, farming out the production of individual components to wherever they can be made at the lowest price, means selling cheaper pencils than the competitor—or getting more profit while maintaining the price, better margins for the same cost. In turn, such sourcing has caused certain industries, particularly specialized ones, to cluster even more tightly together. California's Central Valley, for example, produces some 80 per cent of the world's almonds. Thus, no company—no country—is truly independent, everyone uploaded onto a vast, tangled global network. And that has exposed everyone to new risk. COVID-19 would show that, while individual companies had profited, interdependency had created weakness in the wider ecosystem.

In such a world, with so many moving parts, small shocks in one corner can drastically affect the whole. If war mars Australia, which produces the most iron ore in the world, maybe customers get no toasters in the United Kingdom. If strikes in San Leandro, California, close down the mill, perhaps the American pencil company shuts down. Sometimes that is that. Sometimes the onward impact just stops there. It takes the alignment of millions of stars, millions of dominos falling in just the right way, for small events to ripple big. Most don't, and you never hear about them. Imagine the thousands, maybe millions, of other animal-borne infections all throughout history that, for one reason or another, did not spread so well, their names known only in lab reports and scholarly journals, if at all. The integrated nature of the world, however, combined with instantaneous transmission of information, presents more pathways for these events to escalate—more than ever before. Sometimes, when the San Leandro lumber mill shuts down, it doesn't just affect the pencil company. It could affect the cedar farm in Oregon, too, for one of its biggest clients may be the pencil company that now cannot make pencils.

By the time of COVID-19, China's share of the world economy had become four times the figure during the SARS outbreak. That larger share, when shaken, was enough to send global laptop production plunging by as much as 50 per cent at one point. Four times as big also means four times as connected, in a world already increasingly integrated. A U.S. business is now more likely to sell to China. When that

American business suffers, so does the Canadian company it partners with. So does the French company that buys from the Canadian one. And that's just the ripple effect from the disruption in China alone. When COVID-19 spread, that impact was amplified as economies everywhere shut down. Eventually, European carmakers feared widespread disruption simply because a single electronics manufacturer had been forced to suspend production.

That vulnerability can be seen everywhere, for every small aspect of the economy is a microcosm for the whole, just like how, at the top of a tree, the spindly limbs and their offshoots have the same proportions as the thick trunk and its branches at the bottom. Every branch is a miniature of the one it diverged from, like how, under the microscope, zooming onto bits of a snowflake reveals intricate, repeating patterns. In this complex machine of a world, every cog contains smaller—but just as complex—machines.

Within organizations, roles are so specialized that nobody can do anything by themselves. Even the president of the pencil company has only "a tiny, infinitesimal bit of know-how" on how to make the product, Read wrote in "I, Pencil." To take this a step further, rather than just dividing labour within, companies also parcel it out. For one example, few companies hire their own cleaning staff. Newspapers, for another, increasingly outsource page design to specialized firms. By 2018, a thousand separate American publications had their pages designed out of just twenty-five hubs. At one point, 40 per cent of the world's electronics—iPhones, BlackBerrys, Nokia mobile devices, PlayStations, Xbox, Wii—were contracted out to one Taiwanese company for assembly. Even governments have been increasingly outsourcing. In Alberta, if you lose your driver's licence or want to register a company, it's the private sector that takes care of that. With everyone a gear—not just a part of but also dependent on a greater whole—with everyone occupying such a specialized role in nearly every aspect of society, that creates expansive, pervasive interdependency. Douglas Adams was too generous in saying one person could make even a sandwich from scratch, which would require knowledge in bread-making, animal-rearing, meat-curing, farming, and sauce-blending.

Thus, the ever-present cause and effect, the onward impact of each disturbance to the world, can go on and on and back and forth without end. Eventually, with one-third of humanity under some sort of lockdown, demand for oil fell, and amid an oversupply, the commodity's price hit a negative. Producers had to pay for people to take their crude away. And this doesn't just affect the oil executives—what of the future of cars and those who make them? During the COVID-19 crisis, nobody was visiting shopping malls, restaurants, entertainment venues, or going to school. And services, whatever the kind, make up four in five American jobs. So companies lay off people, who may default on their loans. Companies may default on their loans, too. Bankruptcies quickly started sweeping the retail landscape, with old and respected brands such as Neiman Marcus seeking relief from billions of dollars in debt. Banks took a bludgeoning. Amid the resulting financial uncertainty, everyone spends less, and the cycle repeats. Combine that with supply chain disruptions, the modern world's rapid flow of information, and big finance's high-frequency algorithmic trading (computers now make some 40 per cent of all stock transactions, ensuring business shocks reverberate quickly to investors), and we had a recipe for disaster.

Because of the pandemic, the United States' economy was expected to shrink by a quarter over three months, as large a drop, proportionally, as was seen during the Great Depression over the course of four years, the historian Adam Tooze noted. Unemployment surged to levels not seen since that dark era, increasing by the day, so rapidly that any official figures included here would be outdated—the system can't track them in real time. And around the interconnected world, this picture is replicated—devastation across the land. Just as this medical problem became a financial and economic one, as discontent and frustration mount, it will quickly become a societal and geopolitical one as well. It takes just one rusty cog for the whole system to crash.

A proverb from thirteenth-century Europe—it's nearly impossible to pin its origins more specifically than that—describes how an initially small problem leads into successively more critical stages, resulting in a catastrophic outcome, how tiny fractures grow into chasms. The loss of a single metal pin affected the horse's shoe, and then turned the tide of battle, the proverb reads. "For want of a nail . . . the kingdom was lost."

10

With the massive escalation of events in March had come another disruption to my travel plans: On my return flight from Germany to Canada, I had planned a stop in New Jersey to visit my aunt and two cousins, my Beijing uncle's family. But U.S. president Donald Trump, doing an almost 180-degree about-face from his original laissez-faire attitude about the pandemic, had since decided to ban most travel from the European Union, leaving me out of luck.

My close relationship with my uncle was only strengthened during our week in effective quarantine and symbolically sealed by his giving me his precious last Honeywell H910V face mask. Also, after helping him edit his philosophical essays to his children, I came to know a lot about my uncle's family, whom I hadn't seen for years. So, I had been particularly looking forward to the visit. As I sat in Elias's apartment in Bayreuth, reading the travel-ban announcement from President Trump in sullen frustration, the thought of getting on the phone to change my ticket, yet again, was as pleasant as wet socks. The truth is that I would have much rather tried to touch the moon than spend the next several hours on hold.

When Lieutenant Lewis Nixon, in the 2001 Second World War television series *Band of Brothers,* notices a white flower on the lapel of a dead Wehrmacht soldier, he says: "That's edelweiss. It grows in the mountains, above the treeline, which means he climbed up there to get it." The flower's name is a combination of "noble" and "white" in German, and it blossoms three thousand metres above sea level. According to nineteenth-century lore, young men would risk their lives to retrieve it for their brides. For a warrior, it's a calling card — "supposed to be the mark of a true soldier," Nixon says. But really, the flower's difficulty to obtain was largely an exaggeration by those who plucked it — and that is so especially today, when anyone in the world can order edelweiss online.

The point is, what we previously thought of as exotic and luxurious is now reduced to the commonplace. No doubt, parts of the world are still mired in strife, famine, and poverty, and even the richest and most powerful countries are marred by inequity. But we also live in an unprecedented age, where most in the developed world eat and live better than the king of Bavaria did back in the day. We also have better teeth. And with more than 3.5 billion people around the world owning a smartphone, a piece of machinery that can contain all the world's books and answer pretty much any question you have with the touch of a button, various playing fields have been significantly levelled in the last decade or so. As well, easy and affordable travel between countries has become readily available to more people around the world than we could have imagined even a generation ago. I have gone back and forth around the world, seeing groups of people that in the past would never have met, speaking languages that could not be further from each other. And yet, everywhere, so much has become the same, interchangeable and even mundane. German *gebirgsjäger* troops may still bear the edelweiss insignia, but when what was previously deemed so precious is now ordinary, there is an inevitable loss of meaning in our symbols. In a way, the insignia's greatest significance now is as a reminder of how far we have come.

Globalization, like most things, has its strengths and weaknesses, gains and losses—but, for example, the world no longer erupts into war when a European power annexes part of a neighbour. Now they just sanction the invader. Assassinate an Austrian aristocrat today? Sanction. The closeness of the world has meant that, just as there are companies that profit off bloodshed, there will also always be powerful business interests opposing any all-out war, and that purely economic punishments are deemed harsh enough to deliver the message. We still kill each other, of course, but on nowhere near the scale we used to. More than just enriching parts of the planet and generally bettering people's lives, this interdependence has also been an achievement in the name of peace. Yet it has also made the world painfully vulnerable to a new death. The entire arc of humanity over the past century has bent toward this day of wrath.

The air carried the virus, and between steely wings, it also carried the infected. And more than allowing this rapid contagion-spread, previously unfathomable, globalization also increased the chance that the impacts would ripple, and how widely. Nassim Nicholas Taleb, who wrote *The Black Swan*, has disagreed that this current pandemic is part of the titular phenomenon of his book, an unforeseeable event that causes an impact disproportional to its low probability. To him, it was completely foreseeable. A world like ours, so interconnected, is exactly the sort in which COVID-19 would have such an oversized and paralyzing effect.

The historical parallel of the pandemic to the bubonic plague is uncanny, particularly given that in both cases humanity's own work had made it weak against an unknown threat. The Black Death, too, had come from the East, then a part of the world-spanning Mongol Empire, a pioneer of the west–east Silk Road trade route, which eventually moved the disease as quickly as it did people and goods. Then there were the naval paths of commerce in Europe. It took as little as a year for the plague to spread from Crimea to almost everywhere else in Europe. A 2005 *New Yorker* article read:

> Ironically, the plague is associated with prosperity. As long as a region remains undeveloped, with low populations, small towns, heavy forests, and little trade, its local rats will remain in their holes and die quietly of the plague without passing it.

As the continent developed, as international commerce blossomed and the population doubled, "everything that the Europeans had built up in the preceding centuries turned against them. . . . Their far-flung trade brought them more rats. Their fine cities ran with filth."

This time, it's worse—and not just because our world is more connected. It will also be because it just feels worse, and it feels worse because we do not expect to be so shaken. COVID-19 will likely never kill the millions upon millions that died during the Spanish flu pandemic or at the height of the Black Death. But back then, as the historian Margaret MacMillan noted, people died all the time, women in labour, children in childhood, men at war, and more. Even a stomach infection could be fatal. And life was bitter and socio-economic mobility low. Now, the average life expectancy is just a handful of years under eighty. Even when we die before then, a leading preventable cause is eating too much. The first person to live to 150 has likely already been born. The death toll that would previously have been considered low is now just too much. In our bones and in our blood, our collective state of being is just too tender, for as we built civilization, that civilization, too, has shaped us. We have become built by, and built for, cities and their conveniences, not the frontier and its hardships. From free trade to open borders to instantaneous communications, all that humanity has accomplished has made it vulnerable. Victory has defeated this world.

11

Following my short stay at Elias's apartment in Bayreuth, I went to spend the weekend with family friends not far from where I grew up. Uncle Niu and Aunt Yeung are not actually blood relations of mine, but our families have a bond tempered in the deepest depths, over the hottest coal of the harshest forge: Niu had met my father when he tried to copy off him in university. Or at least that's how my father tells it. I've never heard it from Niu himself. From that allegedly ignoble beginning, the two eventually ended up best friends. Niu and Yeung still live within half an hour of Wuppertal, in the western state of North Rhine-Westphalia, where we had all lived years ago. Niu works at a local university and Yeung runs a chemical company. Niu's daughter, Jeng, a doctor, lives in Hamburg, about a three-hour drive northeast. I was last in Germany in 2018 for her wedding, after which her husband had taken her surname on special request from Niu, whose reasoning was that while his son-in-law has a brother, he has only the one daughter. Niu wanted his surname to live on and be passed to his grandchildren. Jeng's husband—being a modern German with little notion of age-old patriarchal naming conventions—readily agreed. "He doesn't know what he's giving up," Niu joked.

Because of how the virus situation had escalated, Niu had decided to come pick me up, making a five-hour drive south to do so. His reasoning was that he did not want me interacting with strangers and risking infection before arriving at his house. Fair enough, I thought, and it saved me a ten-hour bus ride. It was after sundown when Niu arrived. We had a dinner of large schnitzels at the local pub before handing Risako back the keys to Elias's apartment and heading off. I offered to drive, but Niu declined politely. Being European, Niu had a BMW with manual transmission, and I hadn't driven stick-shift in nearly a decade. I don't even own a car, being the downtown city-dweller I am. And most parts of Germany's Bundesautobahn have no speed limits, a part of the country's cultural identity viewed with awe by outside motoring enthusiasts and with terror by other foreigners. I did not insist on driving.

I had been to Niu and Yeung's red-brick house only when it was being built, in 2006. Conceptually, it was like many North American suburban cookie-cutter homes, mass-produced, newly built, and pretty-looking, yet with no discernible style. But it was a German house, with no front yard and a big backyard, because privacy is more important than image there, and it was a particularly dense structure. You hear no hollowness when knocking on any part of that house. It's good for longevity but not so much for Wi-Fi reception.

I gave Niu and Yeung a bottle of Glenfiddich single-malt whiskey that I'd bought at the Singapore airport duty-free store and some fried fish skin coated with salted egg yolk. I had a great time with them, a welcome respite from the upheaval of COVID-19 and a walk down memory lane in a place that was so close to where I grew up.

Niu had kept a bottle of champagne nearly a quarter-century old, unopened, from the day my father obtained his engineering doctorate. I distinctively remember the party for that event, when my dad was much thinner and had more hair, and was just a little older than I am now. He wore a joke top hat that was a gadget in itself with lots of moving parts, like a wind-up toy—one of those traditions certain professions have for advanced degrees that I am unable to explain any further. A doctorate was a particularly big deal in Germany, which is especially strict on enforcing its law on who can use the honorific "Dr." The bottle of champagne still bore my father's signature and the date. "We'll open it when you get married," Niu told me.

Niu's house is about ten minutes away from Blankenstein Castle, commissioned by Adolf I, Count of the Mark, in the thirteenth century, its main feature being a squarish tower. That town of Hattingen, population 55,000, also has among Germany's best-preserved centuries-old *fachwerkhäuser*—white, timber-framed houses—many of which are uniquely top-heavy, getting wider the higher you go because property taxes were once calculated based on the first storey's square footage. When Yeung and I walked through the downtown, she told me many of those houses have unfortunately become unpopular, at least to their owners. They cannot be demolished due to their heritage status, and the upkeep is prohibitively expensive. In Hattingen's town square, amid the cobblestones, you can still see the medieval pillory for publicly humiliating criminals.

We took leisurely long strolls through the town, which was pleasant and also necessary since the only other thing we really did all weekend was eat. Niu is a big foodie. "I think I will be very happy working as a chef," he said. Yeung is also a great cook, and between them they made slight variations to the dishes I knew, which was always a pleasant surprise. Their *zhajiangmian* noodle dish had come with an egg, yolk still runny, which added to both the consistency and taste. There was a sprinkle of sesame on the *baozi*, which brought a delicate sweetness to the steamed bun with minced-pork-paste filling. Another one of Niu and Yeung's treats was a beef noodle soup, made with a dark broth that included tomato, soy sauce, and the tender parts of the cow that melt in the mouth. I hadn't had it in years, and there was no variation for that one. It tasted almost exactly like what my mother would make. The food, their company, the environment—it was a tonic, something I needed and greatly appreciated.

The next stage of my trip was to meet up with some friends from university, who were coming from Canada. We had discussed such plans for years without actually making them, at least until about half a year earlier when we got serious. Aside from Germany, we intended to go to Ireland and Spain. We had been messaging throughout the crisis, hanging on to our hope that we could still pull it off.

"Real talk tho boys - berlin has about 90 cases or so and with us out and aboot [sic] there's a chance we might catch it," Dillon, with whom I had shared both a university program and student housing, wrote in our group chat, four days before we were due to meet. "How is everybody feeling about it? Feeling lucky like the irish?"

"I dgaf," I wrote, a neutral if vulgar way of saying I had no opinion either way. Our friendship had always been marked by irreverence and dark humour.

Clinton, who had lived in the same student housing as us, said, "If anything, less people in the streets means your [sic] less likely to catch it . . . im going, no way im going back to work." His leave, from a software company, had been applied for and granted. Mentally, Clinton was on holiday. "Ive [sic] already checked out."

"I'm still down to go," Dillon said.

Cameron, Clinton's friend, whom I'd met only once, was down too. Sometimes, things happen for a reason, so you meet them with reason. Sometimes, things happen without reason, so you simply meet them. We had only one dropout: Nick, my former roommate, a software-company project manager, always more level-headed than me.

Two days later, though, while I was with Niu and Yeung, Spain declared a state of emergency, so that country was out. And what seemed like icing on the cake: everyone's company stipulated mandatory work-from-home policies for people who were returning from overseas. Berlin clubs closed. The headline of an *Irish Times* article, posted to the group by Dillon, read, "Ireland is 'exactly 14 days behind Italy' in terms of coronavirus cases." We were still undeterred and decided to pare down the trip to just Ireland. Then Dillon posted another article to the group, in which Canada's foreign affairs minister, François-Philippe Champagne, said, "We recommend that Canadian travellers return to Canada via commercial means while they remain available." Flights were being cancelled, and travel restrictions were going up with little notice. You might be stranded overseas, the government warned. Suddenly, events had escalated way beyond what my friends had a tolerance for:

"Well. Shite," Dillon said. "Sorry guys I think that about does it
for me. At this stage doesn't seem worth [sic] anymore."
Cameron: "Yeah. I don't feel confident in this."
Dillon: "I think we need to postpone this."
Cameron: "Hard to tell if I should cancel or rebook."
Dillon: "I'm waiting until tomorrow to make a decision."
Cameron: "Fun times guys. Makes you feel alive."
Clinton: "Never felt like an adult until today."

And so, my university friends cancelled the trip to Europe, leaving me with a two-week hole in my schedule. I did not try to sway them, never weighing in on their decision-making in the group chat, even though, truth be told, I still wanted them to come. It was not my place to steer them, and I understood their concerns. I knew Minister Champagne, although faintly, having been in some media events with the trilingual lawyer, and once even having a nice conversation with him at the urinal, of all places, and he did not strike me as a man who would give the warning without good reason. Dillon wrote: "We worried that the situation would change more. I'm just wondering if Ireland could turn into an Italy situation. Ireland is okay for now but I'm almost certain that won't be the case in 2 weeks."

It wasn't so much the situation at the time that felt so risky or how truly unprecedented it was, at least in my lifetime. It was how quickly it had become so, which applies whether you look at the small picture or the big—like the economy, every local COVID-19 situation was somehow also a microcosm for the whole. Just a few days ago, everything was all right. The world-famous clubs in Berlin were still open. Then they were not. Spain and Ireland looked totally doable. Then they were not. If everything can change to this extent so rapidly, I thought, sitting in this small town in western Germany with dear old friends, then surely events will escalate at least as rapidly in the days ahead. As the level-headed and, in retrospect, very farsighted Nick said, "These things move quick and exponentially."

12

When an unprecedented crisis like the COVID-19 pandemic meets a world so uniquely sensitive to it, there is only one outcome: society will emerge transformed. We are already seeing social and economic upheavals that have what can only be called a lingering effect. Working from home, demand for delivery, and use of Internet-based entertainment are set to increase. Office-rental, conferences, shopping malls, air travel, tourism, and labour-intensive foods are poised for decline. But the signs are already there for something greater.

Public officials everywhere warn of growing contagion and further restrictions on movement. An Internet publication misquotes the billionaire Bill Gates as saying he envisions chip implants in people showing infection status, and the dubious news spread like a prairie fire, for it's not really that farfetched. Chile had already announced so-called "immunity passports" for people potentially less susceptible to the virus, who will be "freed from all types of quarantine or restriction." Hong Kong slapped trackers on the wrists of those under home quarantine. The device was big and hard to hide, granting it the secondary function of marking people bluntly, like a brightly coloured badge, an anti–immunity passport. If you went out, everyone would know you weren't supposed to. There is nothing more fundamental than the relationship between citizen and state, between people and those who hold power over them, and COVID-19 is set to redefine that balance.

Like most things, at least part of this has to do with money.

In response to the 2008 financial crisis, to put it simply, the dominant solution was for governments to bail out the banks and big corporations. The idea was that when the giants remain afloat, the economy carries on — the money they get trickles down. Yet that did not happen. Not all the money was reinvested in the corporations, passed on to their workers, or pumped back into the economy. American banks were asked to expand lending, but they did not. Their executives did, however, give themselves bonuses of nearly $20 billion. Enforcement of the conditions imposed on bailout money was weak. Within a year, U.S. corporate profits were rising again. And since then, the United States has reduced taxes by about $1.5 trillion, the benefits of which nearly all went to the richest. Whatever little funding was available for helping individuals during the meltdown, such as government programs for mortgage relief, was obscured by disarray, complexity, and deficiency. Societal resentment at the lopsidedness of who benefits built as a result. The top-down approach that assumed giving money to banks and corporations would solve everything was evidently not working. Even until 2015, the median U.S. household income did not climb back to pre-crisis levels. The rise of U.S. president Donald Trump, and to a certain extent, Senator Bernie Sanders, can be directly attributed to this; large swaths of disaffected Middle America resented their various levels of government and voted with that anger.

Perhaps that taught the United States and other countries in the Western world a lesson. In response to the pandemic, there were still the old bailouts, accused of the same faults as before. But governments also decided to try something else: giving ordinary people money, so that they would spend and thus stimulate the economy, bottom-up instead of top-down, doing for the masses what had in the past been done for Wall Street. Across the world, even among those who would consider such a thought anathema not that long ago, the idea of a universal basic income—granting an unconditional periodic payment to everyone—is actually starting to take hold.

It's an old idea. Proponents have said it would be a net benefit: the economy gains when people eschew immediate payoff for future higher-value jobs, instead of worrying about sustenance; reducing problems arising from poverty, such as crime and ill health, means less drain on public resources; and the economy is sustained and society kept at peace when rising automation reduces jobs. But for a long time, universal income had been a fringe concept, among its most prominent champions the one-time U.S. Democratic presidential candidate Andrew Yang; it was popular but had little establishment backing. Then three Democratic senators, two of whom ran against Yang, endorsed a version of that idea. So did Republican U.S. senator Tom Cotton. And Pope Francis, who had been "caged in the library" in Rome. Even the United Kingdom's Conservative prime minister, Boris Johnson, indicated he might consider it.

In countries including Singapore, the United States, and Canada, governments have rolled out widespread income support, with money doled out with few to no restrictions as a direct reaction to COVID-19. With these payments came something else. The Spanish government, an unprecedented alliance of left-wing parties, said it would not only grant basic income but also make it a measure that "stays forever . . . a permanent instrument." A Canadian parliamentarian from the ruling Liberal Party said of his government's pandemic income support, "Hopefully, this is a policy measure that we're able to build on into the future." And he may just get his wish. A taste of basic income isn't quickly forgotten, particularly if people realize that if they had it in the beginning, the pandemic recession would not have been that bad. In countries with those programs, there may just be endurance for some form of universal basic income post-pandemic. It might prove politically difficult otherwise.

That concept of a basic income is just one wave in a bigger tide. It represents a fundamental shift in our view of the role of the government in people's lives—which is markedly increasing. Recall the parallels in past pandemics. The philosopher Michel Foucault said seventeenth-century public health efforts expanded political power drastically, with constant supervision and penalties for noncompliance for communities under lockdown. The plague and its chaos were "met by order." In *Epidemics and the Modern World*, Mitchell Hammond writes that the plague had led to co-operation among city-states such as Florence and Genoa, overriding competitive urges—who knows, maybe today's united Italy had some roots in that pandemic. Cholera and typhoid in the nineteenth century sparked a sanitary movement that resulted in marked increases in urban planning in Western cities, building sewers, enforcing construction codes and maximum occupancies, and paving boulevards and parks, historians have said. Frank Snowden, author of *Epidemics and Society*, has said that even the nineteenth-century sanitary movement helped shape the present-day state. With pandemics, the world becomes a laboratory for greater government, the results of which last even as the experiments pass.

Every time there is a crisis, the governmental arm grows a little. Income taxes were introduced in the First World War in Canada, and Finance Minister Thomas White made a statement that, as the CBC noted, aged badly: "A year or two after the war is over, the measure should be reviewed." In the Second World War, Canada introduced a "baby bonus" payment to parents, a form of which endures to this day. It is, of course, debatable how much change is sparked by any single event, and how much is just the broad sweep of history. There are those who say that, in addition to redrawing the map and defining the international order under which we live, the Second World War also gave birth to the modern European welfare state, as the warfare state of the time had given everyone a taste of big government. For Canada, that conflict birthed its national healthcare system, which never went away. At the time, the *Canadian Public Health Journal* wrote: "Gains must be consolidated. The last war left its lessons. There can be no reduction in public expenditures." Policies introduced during crises, when legislative paths are smoother, are always harder to remove than implement.

That may not always be welcome news. It is hard to argue the sanitary movement of the nineteenth century, in reaction to typhoid and cholera, for example, was anything but good. But the increase of the

State in people's lives can be disconcerting. During COVID-19, from China to Jordan to Serbia to the United Kingdom, governments saw fit to assume new and greater powers. Chile, still reeling from past dissent, declared a "state of catastrophe" and sent soldiers into public squares. Bolivia postponed elections—its last one had been disputed. Filipino lawmakers granted emergency powers to President Rodrigo Duterte, a strongman-type guy who had years ago given police expanded and largely unchecked powers to kill those involved in the country's brutal drug war; who had compared the government's constitution to "toilet paper"; and who had claimed to have personally killed someone as a teen, "just over a look." In Singapore and South Korea, invasive surveillance rose. So did it in Israel, where Prime Minister Benjamin Netanyahu also shut down courts—favourably timed, for he had been scheduled for trial for corruption. That is the same country that instituted a state of emergency during its 1948 War of Independence but never declared it over. Sometimes, there is a large shadow cast by the sheltering hand. Just as how people can acquire a taste for greater social assistance, so, too, can those in power get a stronger whiff of their opiate. Will they ever bear to live without it again?

Even with the creep of the State, many parts of the world are, at the same time, showing a deficit of management, a void for greater government in some form to fill. In the United States, the pandemic has been a blunt reminder of the proper public healthcare it lacks, sticking out sorely among First World countries. In Canada, Vancouver's mayor Kennedy Stewart suggested his city risked bankruptcy unless given a bailout of hundreds of millions of dollars by higher authorities—a story likely to be echoed across the land as residents default on property taxes and fees. In Stockholm, the virus spread through at least 75 per cent of the city's senior care homes, which in recent years have been transferred from state to private management. When the dust settles, something will need to be done about everything, about the services in the hands of lower-level organizations that have either failed or been battered by the crisis. Spain's government—a leftist Socialist Workers' Party allied with the farther-left Podemos—mounted a public take-over of private hospitals. The government in Canada's most populous province of Ontario took over some long-term care homes.

Such takeovers, of course, were happening only in the industrial-ized world, where the State has the power to effect its expansion. Elsewhere, there are governments that already lack control and have become extra-weakened. Nigeria, for example, dependent on oil, an industry disproportionately damned by the pandemic, was on the verge of going broke at the worst possible time. Africa's largest econ-omy had long been battling the Boko Haram Islamist insurgency in the northeast and other violence elsewhere. From where does it find the energy or resources to bother with long-term care homes? For Nigeria and countries like it, with COVID-19, it may become increas-ingly difficult to even keep everything together as before. Then there is the United States, where public trust in the government has been declining for years, a trend all but set to continue among certain quar-ters, which raged against the lockdown measures. Yet, it is precisely the sorts of chaos, division, and uncertainty that will make people crave bigger government, and that collective hunger is a strong force.

In 1920, Denmark's king, Christian X, used his constitutionally granted powers to dismiss his government, ended up nearly overthrown, and never dared to do so again. Power can't just be expanded willy-nilly, even if the law allows it. The real gatekeeper is the people, and their will is what will truly shape the role of government around the world post-pandemic. For countries with weaker governments, that might take longer and it might go along a more twisted path, but it will happen. The current *vox populi* has been shifting, just like in crises of the past.

In the seventeenth century, as Frank Snowden has noted, amid the growing role of the State during the plague, philosophers like Thomas Hobbes and John Locke, considered the founders of modern liberalism, argued citizens needed an authority to protect against the harshness of life. Now we see that idea repeated amid the COVID-19 pandemic, during which the population has seen a gradual shift in collective sentiment, favouring a greater role for governments. "They're part of our survival kit," the scholar Snowden told an interviewer. "And I think the coronavirus shows how quickly life could once again become nasty, brutish, and short without them." Politicians everywhere see their stock rising—even U.S. president Trump, at one point. And, in one poll, the premier of Quebec—whose party clinched power with just 37 per cent of the popular vote—attained 96 per cent approval ratings.

The star of the government is shining even in the strangest of corners, such as among people in cryptocurrency, usually known for their anti-state, individualistic bent. Bitcoin was created in the wake of the 2008 financial crisis, and the community and multi-billion-dollar sector had traditionally leaned libertarian and toward the tiniest of small government. Now, according to a reader survey from the industry publication *CoinDesk*, strong majorities favour state-enforced measures like physical distancing, travel restrictions, and telling corporations what to manufacture. Just like the saying that there are no atheists in foxholes, there are few libertarians in pandemics, and like everything else that happened amid the crisis, this will leave a mark. With COVID-19, we are moving toward a world in which, perhaps, the term "bureaucracy" will have less of a negative connotation.

After my stay at Uncle Niu's, with most of my plans cancelled, I returned to Elias's apartment in Bayreuth. I again met Risako at the train station, walking once more the same cobblestones and the streets paved with rock carved from the Fichtel Mountains to the east. I spent a lot of time hanging out with her in the subsequent days. We had drinks together and went for walks sometimes, as all around us, the restrictions on movement became tighter.

On the last day that restaurants were allowed to open, we resolved to go to one. I hadn't been to one since Singapore, and that felt like a lifetime ago. I had been eyeing this one place that served the German delicacy *currywurst*—sausage served with a special spiced ketchup. It's funny the curry from the dish isn't derived from any contact with Asia, like how the British got their taste for the spice. The Germans actually got it *from the British*, from occupying soldiers after the Second World War. The dish is now so German that Volkswagen, which has its own butchery for it, makes more sausages than cars. *Currywurst* is definitely not high cuisine, but I must have it at least once any time I go to Germany, and when I saw it on the menu of what looked like a really fancy restaurant, that stoked my interest all the more.

Unfortunately, Risako and I never ended up having it. We never ended up going to any restaurant. In the previous days, the restaurants

were having their hours restricted, and many closed of their own voli-
tion due to the lack of customers. Risako and I couldn't find any sit-
down eatery that was open and ended up at a *döner kebab* stand Elias
had recommended.

So, we sat by the river, the Red Main rushing black into the night.
The stars were soft and blurry, almost faded, and half-covered by
clouds. Beneath them, the streetlamps accented the foil around our
imperial beef-wrap feast, the yellow of the light dancing upon crinkled
silver, and the wind blew from the north, brisk and boundless. It was
only the second day of spring, the season so young, it seemed reluctant
to relinquish the winter. It took only a few bites of the *döner* to acknowledge the riverside was too cold. We went back indoors.

I think when language is restricted, you have to try harder to speak
more plainly, which ironically makes communication more forthright.
When Risako sometimes couldn't find the right English words, I would
try to finish her sentences, eventually describing her thoughts almost
as if I were reading her mind. The accurateness tickled both of us.
Soon, though, our meetings became technically illegal. You were only
allowed to congregate with people in your own household, the state
government said. "The police will be under an obligation to check
compliance," read a "Decree" from the southeastern state of Bavaria.
Our little rendezvous became a dirty deed, clandestine meetings under
what Elias would only half-jokingly describe as "martial law."

Unlike how I would have imagined it, there was no stark line crossed
or major happening to mark these new restrictions on civil liberties.
They came into my world muted and unaggressive, no comet to mark
their birth. They simply existed, a new normal creeping in without

fanfare, the way the sun dawns and the tide breaks. Like the Italians just two weeks earlier, I went to sleep one night and woke up in the future.

And what a future it was to be. Even as government size inched outward, even as the world writhed and morphed under an unequalled calamity to which it was and is uniquely helpless, an even greater transformation loomed. The full impact of this bat-borne plague had yet to be felt.

PART FOUR
DEATH OF A (GLOBAL) VILLAGE

13

Elias's apartment sat on a row of uniform sandstone buildings with red-tile roofs, on a rock-paved boulevard developed in the eighteenth century, in the dying days of the Holy Roman Empire which, up until 1806, nominally held together much of the continent. It was kind of like the European Union of its day. The road on which Elias's apartment sat was called Friedrichstraße. There's a street in every German city with that name, Berlin's being its major culture and shopping hub. They're like the multitudes of Avenue Victor Hugo in France, except the specific Fred that each is named after isn't always as clear. You'd think they're all based on Frederick the Great, arguably the most famous Fred, but not so—there was just less of a selection of names back then. Berlin's street was actually named after the Great's grandfather. Bayreuth's Friedrichstraße was developed under the local ruler, the Great's brother-in-law, also called Frederick—who once owned the address at which Elias lived (before Mozart's cousin moved in, by the way). Called a margrave, a bit like a prince, the local ruler had an uncle also called Frederick. The German Romantic writer Jean Paul, whose statue stands at the intersection of Bayreuth's Friedrichstraße and Ludwigstraße, also had Frederick somewhere in his name.

The *ch* in Friedrich does not make a hard sound like a *K*, which I learned because, as we walked down Friedrichstraße's stony tiles one day, Risako, ever the Germanic-literature student, made sure to correct my pronunciation. It's "Freed-*r'sch*," she said. That, combined with, in quick succession, yet another unexpected *sch*-sound and a throaty, back-of-mouth guttural *R* in "straße," really makes the street name a quintessential German challenge.

In Bayreuth, I lived in social limbo. I had only one source of real-life human contact, Risako. But being someone who likes solitude, I've never been bored by boredom. I've never minded the company of silence and thoughts. If I were at all religious, and could endure celibacy, I would have seriously considered becoming a monk. I had come, unexpectedly, to like the idea of having weeks of nothing in my schedule; it was a forced hiatus I never knew I needed.

There was a certain familiarity I felt toward Bayreuth, even though, prior to this trip, I had never been to the city in my life. It was Germany, and that was enough. Aside from that brief visit in 2018 for the wedding of Niu and Yeung's daughter, I hadn't been back to the country for more than a decade. Everything in Bayreuth was a source of comfort, even—or perhaps, particularly—the little things. Elias's apartment had an old-style German toilet, one with a "continental-shelf" construction in the white bowl. Out of politeness, I will refrain from over-describing, but it was the sort I hadn't seen for years, and it brought an odd sense of nostalgia.

I gorged myself on the two favourite foods I had as a child: *schwein-skopfsülze*, a sweet and vinegary meat jelly made with pig's head (yes, I know how this sounds), eaten cold, and Hanuta wafers, with thick hazel-nut cream between layers. All my life, I considered these foods the rarest of treats — as a child, when my parents controlled my diet, and as an adult, when I would get them only via care packages from Niu and Yeung. There are limits to the benefits of globalization. The latter can be found for ten times the price on Amazon. The former — well, I think aside from me and three weirdos, nobody outside of Europe wants anything to do with meat jelly made from pig's head. I know it's the twenty-first century, and anything can be found anywhere if you have the will, but mine isn't that strong. So now, in Bayreuth, when I got to have them every day, well, I was as happy as a kid on Halloween. I started stockpiling the foods. I had space in my luggage and had resolved to bring as much back to Canada as I could get away with.

A week in, I gritted my teeth to call the airline and rebook my ticket back to Canada; the one that originally routed through the United States was now effectively null and void due to U.S. travel restrictions. I brought my return to Toronto forward by two weeks. Might as well, I thought. Then, days later, my flight got cancelled again. As it turned out, Air Canada had decided to stop flying the route, so back on the phone I got, navigating the jammed lines as best I could, the sort of call for which you need to stiffen the sinews and summon the blood.

In every old western movie, there comes a point when the protago-nist has a chance to leave town unharmed, ride into the sunset. But for whatever reason — a moment of clarity, a need to see things through, or even a death wish — he ends up staying, perhaps against his better judgement. In Bayreuth, I ended up doing something I previously never expected to do: I postponed my return to Toronto by more than two weeks from the original date. This could certainly be construed as sheer folly, ignoring all the government warnings—not to mention plain common sense—to get back to your own country before getting shut out for God knows how long. But while the situation was certainly changing wildly by the day, it was obvious to me at this point that going back to Canada wouldn't offer much of anything anyway. With the lockdown measures, I'd be more or less isolated there too, prevented from seeing most people—no pubs, no in-person meetings, no friends, no nothing. My intention with this trip in the first place, besides getting to see my ailing grandfather, my parents, and some friends, was to disappear for a while and take a break. Holing up in my friend's empty apartment, in a small town in southern Germany, without a whole hell of a lot to do fit the bill nicely.

I knew full well that in feeling what I felt and doing what I did, I was also trying to hold on to something, yearning for the familiar amid the strange, aching for an ever-distant past that was increasingly no more than a memory. Eventually, I would find that none of the comfort to be derived from this quaint little town could shield or even distract me from what was going on in this country, this continent, and the world. But for a little while, at least, I felt at ease, protected by the sandstone walls and cobblestone streets around me and my memories of better, simpler times.

Crises reveal true mettle. With unprecedented speed, the pandemic and Europe's traumatic and widely varied responses to it had made it all the more apparent that the continent I knew and had grown up with was fading. There was something disturbing about this, like the Bayreuth ravens that flew low amid the heavy air and the Arctic gust across the black North Sea. Even in a new season, the winter casts its shadow—a dark implication beyond the tug of sentimentality, a foreboding outside the bounds of present dread. Beneath my feet, amid the plague, my world was shifting.

And it wasn't shifting back.

14

Elias had told me to check out the ubiquitous Euroshop, which, as he explained, wasn't a souvenir chain emblematic of the continent, as I had thought, but a discount store where everything sells for one euro or thereabouts. He said it was full of funny little trinkets, although he once found bottles of wine there. I called upon one Euroshop only to find it closed, for it was not considered an essential business. Downtown Bayreuth was rife with shuttered shops. As I strolled the Friedrichstraße that led to it, sometimes with Risako, sometimes alone, I watched the crowds grow progressively thinner in an increasingly desolate downtown.

Sometimes, Risako and I would walk in the gardens outside Margrave Frederick's palace, now a museum. We passed chestnut and oak trees, squirrels darting between. The canal water was always still and green as the grass, the gravel grinding beneath our feet—and the blue playground sealed off by red-and-white tape, another stark reminder that this little German haven was not untouchable.

The thought did cross my mind to disregard the barrier and have a walk through the playground, maybe even push myself off from the swings. I figured that we were already breaking one rule: our strolls, of course, were *verboten*. The mingling of people from different households was technically illegal. But while you can't tell what households two people are from by just looking at them, it is easy to discern by sight that someone is using a playground unauthorized. I recalled the "Decree" from the state of Bavaria, saying police will "check compliance," and decided to let thoughts remain just thoughts. Indeed, perhaps because fewer people were outside, I started noticing the cops more. The police-to-civilian ratio in Bayreuth, as in Beijing when I was there, was definitely getting higher.

At the palace garden, all Risako and I could do was walk along the hedges and shrubs, which looked shabbier by the day. We couldn't go inside the museum itself, for it had been closed as well. They say much of it was personally designed by Margrave Frederick's wife, Princess Wilhelmine of Prussia, who accepted the marriage only after being strong-armed by her father the king, also a Frederick. But I would never know.

One day, it snowed in spring, ice crystals faintly falling upon the yellow-brown sandstone, on the red-tile roofs and the hard streets paved with mountain rock, and on the black-metal statue of Jean Paul, and the rushing Red Main River, and all that is Bayreuth. Despite the drastically different history, smaller scale of the town, and the different language of the citizens, it reminded me vividly of Beijing, of the night I walked between the snowflakes.

But that's where the similarities ended. While the crisis had hit a rising China, it had landed on an increasingly unstable, downward-trending Europe. Plagued as it already was by the British exit from the European Union, an out-of-control refugee crisis, rising political polarization and populism, and an annual economic growth hovering around 2 per cent in its best years, Europe had its guard down when COVID-19 came knocking. Despite the common market, national leaders hoarded and scrambled for medical supplies. Italy, whose infections soon outstripped China's, complained it had been abandoned. "European solidarity does not exist," Serbian president Aleksandar Vučić told his country. Serbia's not in the EU, but its joining the bloc had been in the works for more than ten years. Continental unity is nothing more than "a fairy tale," Vučić said. For Europe, the pandemic was cinderblocks on already sinking feet.

Risako's parents back home started worrying about her, the only girl in a brood of boys. So did her university in Japan (she was in Bayreuth for a year of study abroad). Like Canada, pretty much every other country in the world was calling in its citizenry before the doors potentially slammed shut. Risako's dormitory mate, a tall Swede called Ludvig who was about double her size, was going back to his home country, but Risako herself did not seem overly concerned. She half-joked to me that Asian people probably have a higher tolerance to the virus since we're from where it originated. She had a whole other semester of school in Bayreuth to attend, and she really could not have been in a more perfect place as a student of Germanic studies. (Long before

Wagner, long before the town became a centre of Nazi ideology, its rulers, Frederick and Wilhelmine, built the town into what was then an intellectual hub of Western Europe, almost like a modern-day Cambridge.) In the end, Risako resolved to stay. She was happy in Bayreuth, and who could blame her?

On the other hand, Elias resolved to stay away. He was, in fact, caught in COVID-19 lockdown mid-travel, and much like me, his plans were far from straightforward. Elias had gone from Bayreuth to Canada, but between the two he made a stopover in Finland, where his grandparents and father live and where he had once gone to school—a home base he visits often. Elias's return route, from Canada to Bayreuth, was again to be via Finland, where he had planned to stay for a little while. But now, with COVID-19, he had to be isolated for two weeks when he got back to Finland. Like the rest of the world, borders had gone up across Europe, with most countries effectively banning non-residents. Being a student at the local university, Elias could still get into Bayreuth, but he was anticipating potentially more lockdowns and further worsening of the virus situation. I had told Elias about all the disruptions to my travel plans, but that I eventually sorted everything out and had a ticket back to Canada, to which he responded, "For now." Instead of returning to Germany, Elias opted to just remain indefinitely in his Nordic land.

Elias's university was moving to online classes anyway, and unlike me, he never had much affinity for Germany. Sometimes, the whole country frustrated him, starting with the Munich Airport, where he once got lost. To Elias, Germany was a land of many unusual rules, which it expected foreigners to just instinctively know. To top it off, Elias looks like a German—like someone for whom there is an even bigger expectation to know how everything works. Unfortunately, Elias's Finnish furlough effectively meant that after all this, he and I would miss each other. I was saddened by that. I would have loved to have seen him.

The backdrop to Elias's exile, the unprecedented travel restrictions in the Schengen no-border zone, represented a paralysation of movement, an immobility that ran counter to the free passage of people and goods that is one of the hallmarks of the EU. Elias hadn't bought any tickets in advance for the Finland–Germany leg of his trip he eventually cancelled because he figured he was fine to just buy them closer to the day of travel. Continental flights were like taking the bus. On the ground, millions of Europeans commute to work across borders every day. People can live in Zgorzelec but work in Görlitz, or Lafelt–Maastricht, or Bratislava–Vienna. The Greater Luxemburg region includes three other countries. I have an uncle in Switzerland, and when I was at his place last, we casually popped over to Germany for dinner. Between twenty-six continental countries, there were no immigration barriers, even when flying; officials could conduct only security checks. But now, the uniquely continental free-movement bloc, emblematic of all that is Europe, was shut tight with little notice. Just like that.

No doubt, people working in other countries or with good reason to travel could still do so, and the lockdown of the Schengen zone, no matter how long, will eventually lift. But the basic premise, that travel should be free unless there is justification to the contrary, had now been reversed. And the simple fact that it had happened—not impossible, but definitely unthinkable in the past—established the closing of borders as something that could happen again. Beyond the continent, the meaning of this closure is largely symbolic, but symbols matter. This is a part of a bigger issue, a greater upheaval in Europe and greater change in the world still to be wreaked by the pandemic. Symbols are, after all, manifestations of the arc of history, or as German historian Oswald Spengler referred to them, the "emblematical impression of the Cosmos upon us."

Nostalgia runs deep in Bayreuth, immeasurable and bottomless, beyond its pride in the composer Richard Wagner and the opera house he built 150 years ago. Its well-preserved architecture, for which Margravine Wilhelmine was almost singlehandedly responsible, emphasizes grandeur. Domes were common in its Rococo style, with interiors painted with angels and sculpted sunbeams. Stairways were prominent, grand, and used for dramatic effect. Visitors looked to the ceilings and saw the heavens. Walking around town, if you suspend disbelief for a moment, it's almost as if you're back 300 years ago, in the intellectual hub of the Holy Roman Empire. But of course, Wilhelmine's largesse in building Bayreuth had nearly bankrupted the local government. And by that time, the Holy Roman Empire, in the famous words of the French philosopher Voltaire, who visited Bayreuth sometimes, was "in no way holy, nor Roman, nor an empire"—only a failed attempt to relive glory from classical antiquity. In a way, the illustrious past Bayreuth evokes is a bit hollow, itself an attempt to evoke an even more distant past. Everything about it exuded a painful longing, tragically to be unfulfilled. Sometimes, the sweetness of nostalgia is only in its unattainable taste.

"Is that Wagner?" I would ask Risako every time we'd see a statue or bust. We had a joke between us, in which I would ask her random questions about the town, like how old this or that building was, or what the significance was behind the big dinosaur statue downtown, and when she'd inevitably draw a blank on it, I'd say: "You're supposed to know this. Isn't this what you study?"

Somehow, in this Wagnerian town, it was never Wagner, with his chin-strap neckbeard like a pulled-down face mask. Alas, the Bayreuth Festival honouring Wagner, which began in 1876 and is organized by the composer's descendants, had been cancelled for 2020 due to the pandemic.

I learned from Risako that Ludvig, who had deposited his stuff at the apartment where I was staying while he went back to Sweden, had contracted COVID-19. He was infected by someone in his family upon returning home, but I didn't know that at first. At the time, every time I looked at Ludvig's cardboard boxes, thin mattress, ironing board, leather messenger bag, and his poster of the nineteenth-century German painting "Wanderer above the Sea of Fog" by Caspar David Friedrich, a pale and tendril-like thought gripped me: could I have caught the plague? From boxes? A mattress?

I began to grow sad in Bayreuth as the days went by, amid the pandemic and lockdown. I felt that sad was the most appropriate feeling, really, though that thought just made me even sadder. Sadness, to me, is not the strongest sentiment among the negative emotions, but it does feel like it's the most final. Anxiety is uncertainty about future events. Fear is aversion to harm. Anger is reaction to provocation. Every one of these prompts further action. But sadness—pure, saturated sadness, and nothing else—is felt only when you know there is no solution to the situation. Sadness sparks no onward effect. It is anxiety realized. It is fear met, unfruitfully. It is anger drained and spent. Sadness begets only acceptance. It means finality, that what was in the past, what was lost, will never again be regained.

One Wednesday, I cracked open a beer and sat to watch a rare event: German chancellor Angela Merkel addressing her nation on television. She normally gave such speeches only on New Year's Day.

I had a Kaiserkrone lager, a six-pack of which sold for a little over one euro. German bottles are also bigger, a full pint instead of twelve ounces, perfect for watching a political speech during a pandemic. And Merkel did not disappoint. Having been chancellor for nearly fifteen years, the former scientist (with a doctorate in quantum chemistry) was the longest-serving head of government in the European Union. Merkel was straightforward, empathic, and transparent, a leader and a stateswoman. "This is serious," she said of the virus. "Take it seriously." One blemish on Merkel's speech, I thought, was her focus on her own people.

That inwardness might have been expected from the leader of, say, Estonia, but Germany is the EU's biggest economy, and Merkel had long been the de facto leader of the bloc, and as such, other countries looked to her for guidance. Yet her speech made no mention of the continent's common struggle. Europe was not mentioned even once. In fact, when the camera was zoomed in, which was most of the time, the EU flag to the far left of Merkel disappeared. Even when it was on screen, the flag was never fully in frame. Days later, it was Germany's president, a largely ceremonial leader, who called for continental solidarity.

Even then, with most European leaders gazing inward at their public-health and economic crises, just like Merkel, I wondered who even had the attention span to listen. They did heed the German president's words eventually, with various forms of aid flowing from the less to the more affected countries, but the trickle of solidarity was slow, and COVID-19's spread was anything but. France and Germany's proposed 500-billion-euro recovery fund came nearly three months after the first lockdowns in Italy. I couldn't help but think that the onslaught of the virus across the continent could have been a time to shine for the Union, a chance to flex its collaborative muscles after Brexit, after the rise of populism in some of its states, and to demonstrate to the world what unity and co-operation looks like. For all its myriad faults, the EU had had a purpose as a force for stability, a bulwark against disturbance and a champion of multilateralism. The EU had been an anchor for the so-called liberal international order—the alliances, institutions and rules-based system dominated by Western democracies and their values—the framework for global engagement and the very structure under which we all live. European chaos in the face of the virus, the lack of a coherent collective response, the competition for medical equipment, and the hesitation of the steadier countries to help carry the devastated, is both a symptom and a cause —both symbol and constituent factor—of the unravelling of that order.

Since the end of the Second World War, there has existed a web of bilateral agreements, military alliances and trade pacts, and international bodies such as the United Nations, the World Court, the World Trade Organization, the International Monetary Fund and, yes, the World Health Organization. This structure is loose and subjectively defined, but generally observers have dubbed it the "liberal international order," the small-l "liberal" referring not to the traditional political left, but its dictionary definition of openness. It is based on fair play and adherence to equally and consistently applied rules, upheld by Western democracies and their armies who do not always adhere to those rules. That order had sprouted out of the ravages of war, when the newly risen United States built up the battered Europe through its Marshall Plan aid and planted military bases around the world that stand to this day.

The twenty-first century, however, with its waves of conflicts and crises, discord and political extremes, had been deleterious to Europe. Meanwhile, since 2017, the United States under President Donald Trump had turned increasingly inward and hostile toward international partners and obligations, bending toward ataxia and abdicating its traditional world-leadership role. "International relationships that had seemed immutable for 70 years are being called into question," Canada's then–foreign affairs minister Chrystia Freeland told Parliament in 2017. "From Europe, to Asia, to our own North American home, long-standing pacts . . . are being tested." Those long-standing pacts and immutable relationships—that system and structure—are deeply flawed, to be sure. The West-led order, backed by military dominance, is not unlike the empires of old. But it also granted stability and a framework for international engagement that had brought the world closer and more tightly integrated. For those willing to embrace it, such as Canada, the empire had, according to Freeland, "formed the bedrock of our security and prosperity."

Now, as that bedrock weakens, as those upholding the empire no longer do so as steadfastly, challengers to the world order have grown more assertive. China aggressively pursued territorial claims in Asia and waged a wide control-and-influence campaign in Africa. Russian rifles rode high into the Middle East and Eastern Europe. Observers also pointed to an escalating intelligence war, not seen since the Cold War. Long before the pandemic, the path of the international order as we knew it had already been unsteady. Pungent-sweet and high-octane as it may be, the virus was only an accelerant for a world stage that, for years, had already been on fire.

15

When he eventually arrived in Finland from Canada, Elias sent me a picture of himself with the wildest, bushiest bushman red beard I have ever seen on him or anyone else. Finland, as it turned out, was the perfect place to be during a pandemic. It is remote, relatively under-populated, stable, and has consistently ranked at the top of the World Happiness Report (yes, there is such a thing). And Elias managed to find a cabin by a lake that was so remote, there is literally only one result when you Google its name. There, Elias spent his time fishing and farming in the woods of southeastern Finland, far from major cities, near ancestral lands and stony, moss-ridden ruins of old churches, at least one of which dated back to the fifteenth century. While Elias had family nearby, he lived mostly alone. Oftentimes, there was nothing else moving but the water, the birds above, and the sun and moonlight dancing on the lake's surface. Elias was far from the chaos of the world. "I don't know what it is, but something about sitting here in the beauty, abundance, and depth of nature makes me suspicious of the very concept of progression, ambition, and ego itself. I need one fish and some plants each day, firewood and a roof. That's it," he told me. "If everyone saw the world and life like this, there would be no need for countries, politics, or armies. . . . If humans were peaceful, nurturing, cuddly monkeys that had no predators and that attempted no empires."

There's a Chinese saying, though, that when the tiger abdicates the mountain, the monkey reigns. Not so far from Elias's forest seclusion, the world amid COVID-19 was going in a completely different direction from the one he sought. In crises, there are those who delve inward, who seek seclusion and removal. But there are also those who look outward at all the chaos around them and see opportunity. As the Roman emperor Marcus Aurelius writes, "What stands in the way becomes the way."

When the United States announced in April 2020 that it was going to cut funding to the 194-member World Health Organization (WHO) over its handling of the pandemic, China stepped right in, increasing its contribution by $50 million. China sent its European Union ambassador to a global meeting to fund a vaccine, while the United States declined to participate. China did not make a financial contribution to that $8-billion effort, and its gift to the WHO was far from the $400 million the United States gave in 2019. But the optics of those moves were enough. China was more than happy to be seen stepping up its support of an international organization while the U.S. was stepping down. And those moves were only the beginning.

Hong Kong, the former British colony and current global financial hub, is supposed to be governed differently from mainland China, with more freedoms and different, more liberal laws. In 2019, protests involving millions of people broke out, sparked by Beijing's attempt to alter that status quo, extending further control by introducing extradition laws so that errant residents could be prosecuted under mainland justice. The movement intensified on the seventieth anniversary of Communist rule in China, and the first Hong Kong protestor to take a bullet during these widespread protests was shot that October 1 of 2019. With the world watching, the broken storefronts, fistfights, and mass arrests put Beijing in a bind. The protestors were able to squeeze concessions from the authorities, to the point that Hong Kong leader Carrie Lam contemplated resignation.

Now, though, with the virus, it quickly became apparent that one situation's problem was another's solution. Near the end of January, the city had imposed a state of emergency, ostensibly to deal with the pandemic, even though the region had only five confirmed cases of the virus at the time, all of which were found in people who had visited Wuhan. There is no question COVID-19 measures were necessary, and the Hong Kong government had been under fire for reacting slowly, but banning gatherings of more than four people was also the perfect solution to curbing the protests. Authorities eventually arrested fifteen protest leaders, a move that would have invited massive backlash and chaos in the streets if it had happened before COVID-19. Now, the student-activist Joshua Wong, the de facto face of the movement, said on a podcast that the containment measures made it "impossible for us to mobilize." Then came the finishing move. Beijing introduced a new national security law in Hong Kong against what it deemed treason, sedition, and secession—effectively a move to take complete control. Demonstrators planned to march again, but with the world engulfed by the virus, even as Western leaders condemned the new law, hardly anyone else was watching. Since 2019, Beijing had held off on such daring salvos in Hong Kong, perhaps mindful of the international backlash after troops opened fire on Tiananmen Square protestors in 1989. Now, it had found its moment. Also amid the pandemic, a top Chinese general said his country would not rule out using military force to take back Taiwan, a territory China claims, which has long had U.S. support. On the heels of pestilence, the clarion of war.

And China never forgets. The Asian giant is the land of the long game, the proud "Middle Kingdom" of the world, the literal translation of its name, "middle" not referring to middling-ness but to a prime, central position. Beginning over 150 years ago, China had suffered what it called a "century of humiliation," losing wars with outside powers that are forever etched into national memory. Like its attempt to control the South China Sea and the triple-digit-billions of dollars it poured into African infrastructure, Beijing's initial creep into Hong Kong represented an outward push, growing and expanding, trying to impose a new hegemony onto the world and avenge the humiliations of ages past. It was distilled into a message attributed to the founding father Mao Zedong, with his heavy Hunan regional accent, all the way back when the People's Republic was founded in 1949: "The Chinese people have stood up."

That need to rectify perceived past slights is a powerful motivator. Once one of two global superpowers, the Soviet Union collapsed at the end of the Cold War. Then an intelligence officer in East Germany, Vladimir Putin was deeply affected by those events. When he became president in 1999, he wrote, "Russia faces the real danger that it could be relegated to the second, or even the third tier." So, in Putin's two-decades-and-counting of effective power, evidence mounted of Russia's overseas assassinations, hacking, annexation of Crimea, military intervention in the Middle East, and interference in Western elections. Putin would make repeated denials, but there is no question that everything he does draws from the same reserve, from that moment in history when his beloved country fell, defeated by the West—not that different from China. To be sure, Russia has much military and intelligence might, but little so-called soft power. Its economy is not even in the world's top ten, ranking just below Canada's. Moscow thus has less to gain from the pandemic than Beijing. But in the turbulence of COVID-19, Russia too saw opportunity, and reportedly, it did what it does best.

Disinformation, even as Russia repeatedly denies any use of the tactic, has its roots in the Soviet Union. The term is, in fact, a loanword from there, adopted from the Kremlin, although it is not inherently Russian. The term comes from *dezinformatsiya*, which is itself a form of disinformation, coined in that way by Russia to suggest Western origin. (The leader Joseph Stalin allegedly thought it French-sounding.)

In the age of COVID-19, a leaked European Union document disclosed that Russia had been disseminating fake news online in English, French, German, Italian, and Spanish, using conflicting and confounding reports to complicate the bloc's dissemination of its COVID-19 response. According to the document, "The overarching aim of Kremlin disinformation is to aggravate the public health crisis in Western countries . . . in line with the Kremlin's broader strategy of attempting to subvert European societies." China had allegedly been doing the same thing—learning from Russia, in fact. According to analysis by the Alliance for Securing Democracy, a project of the German Marshall Fund of the United States, Beijing had been signalling a "move toward a more Russian style of information manipulation." The Chinese allegedly boosted existing conspiracy theories and also drew from campaigns by Russia and Iran. A *ProPublica* investigation found co-ordinated Twitter accounts had posted about Beijing's glorious triumph and leadership amid the pandemic—part of a ten-thousand-strong network. China's moves make it "clear that a new era of disinformation has dawned," a Freedom House analysis reads. China has denied acting improperly, a stance it holds so strongly that it reportedly tried to stop an EU report on Beijing's disinformation and ended up getting the bloc to water it down. Yet, the covert aside, plain as a pike, the world could see Chinese senior officials and state media spreading suggestions on social media that the United States was responsible for the coronavirus.

Sowing disinformation is simple. The Internet and our digital connectivity have made it easier to reach the masses, and the masses are gullible. Research shows most American students, from middle school to even university, can't tell the difference between real news and propaganda. The essence of disinformation, for the most part, isn't to steer people in any particular direction, but simply to sow chaos and disunity. Such division causes a loss of trust and faith in institutions. It is destabilizing. It can and does weaken the receiving countries, for poison in the mind often manifests in directions that even the trolls may not expect. It does not take a lot to swing elections, with the results of many districts decided by tiny margins. In 2016, it did not take a lot for an American to fire a gun in a pizza parlour in which he incorrectly believed children were being sexually abused by Democratic Party members. A lot can hinge on memes and tweets, on robot social media accounts, and on rumour and manipulated photos. Now, more than ever before, a face can truly launch a thousand ships.

Then, of course, there is the good ole traditional spy craft. Two Canadian intelligence agencies said "it is near certain that state-sponsored actors have shifted their focus during the pandemic" and warned of "an increased risk of foreign interference and espionage." They didn't specify from what countries the hostile moves would come, but in the past, one agency had more than once accused China and Russia of such activities.

And for China in particular, hand in hand with the disinformation and intelligence work came the medical aid and protective gear it had been handing out around the world. When Germany and France responded to the pandemic by restricting exports of protective equipment, sparking backlash from neighbours, China was reaching outward in what observers have called "face mask diplomacy." China prominently publicized what it portrayed as aid sent to the hard-hit Italy. From Spain to France, and to the Czech Republic—the Asian country capitalized on the public-relations moments as well. It may be cynical to overly analyze goodwill, but then again, Spain later complained the Chinese test kits it bought from a private company didn't work. The results of Beijing's overtures are clear for all to see. Serbia's president Aleksandar Vučić said of the pandemic, "The only country that can help us is China." Italy's ambassador to the European Union said when his country asked for help with protective medical equipment: "Not a single EU country responded. . . . Only China responded bilaterally. Certainly, this is not a good sign of European solidarity." China looked like a rescuing hero, eclipsing the old world leader, the United States—which was also on the receiving end of Chinese charity, with a donation of test kits and masks by the billionaire co-founder of Alibaba, Jack Ma.

Beneath everything runs an economic crusade. Given the accusations of China's enforced wall of silence during the earliest known spread of COVID-19, and of similar actions during the SARS epidemic, what the country presents as its progress in its fight against the virus should be examined critically and in context. But what is clear is that when everyone else was still reeling from the effects of COVID-19, China, which dealt with it swiftly and accordingly, was already restarting its economy as other countries were shutting theirs down. "Beijing intends to use the global dislocation and downturn to attract foreign investment, to seize strategic market share and resources . . . to, as Chinese sources put it, 'leap-frog' industrially," reported an analysis by Horizon Advisory, a consultancy focused on China. This was amid economic devastation almost everywhere else, beyond just the United States. The north of Italy, the country's hardest hit region, accounts for 50 per cent of the economy. Germany's economy shrank by 2.2 per cent in the first three months of 2020, the sharpest quarter-on-quarter decline since the 2008 financial crisis. The American billionaire financier George Soros said the European Union could disintegrate in the wake of the new coronavirus outbreak unless the bloc makes certain drastic economic measures. Horizon Advisory's analysis pulled no punches when it stated, "In COVID-19, Beijing sees the chance to win." How far the country can go, how effectively China can take advantage of the situation, remains to be seen. Far more certain, though, is that the further rise of players like China will be at the expense of the West. This is not a value judgement, but a dispassionate statement of the times—and one with certain consensus. Research from the University of Calgary reads: "Moscow also views the virus as a fortuitous harbinger of the end of the post–Cold War liberal world order."

I took up running while staying in Bayreuth, although I've never been much of a runner. My choice of exercise is rock climbing, which I try to do three times a week, being a bit of an obsessive. If I'm in a city for more than two weeks, I have to find a local facility to visit. But with the pandemic, the lone climbing gym in Bayreuth was closed. So, if I was to stay in any kind of shape, I was forced to take up running. I didn't even have the shoes, having packed only one pair of leather boots for the whole trip. I had to buy off-brand runners from a discount supermarket, the only place that sold shoes and was allowed to remain open. They were fifteen euros and purple, not my favourite colour, but Risako said they looked "nice." Personally, I didn't think they were worth even five euros. I suspect they were of slightly different sizes and, as such, my feet constantly ached in them, particularly the left one. By the end of my first long run down Wittelsbacherring (a street named after the House of Wittelsbach, the clan of King Ludwig II), I was exhausted, and my feet throbbed. I longed to get back to a time where I could resume my rock climbing, a discipline that's far easier on the body, believe it or not.

The most common gyms in Germany, by a wide margin, are called McFit, whose slogan, translated from the German, is "Simply Look

Good." They're cheap, plentiful, and open at all hours of the day and night, not unlike the GoodLife chain in Canada. In North America, the *Mc* prefix is used pejoratively (like in "McMansion," to describe mass-produced houses of low quality), evoking the U.S. restaurant chain McDonald's. The negative connotation clearly did not make it cross the Atlantic, and while funny, it's not surprising. Germans, I've always felt, love the United States. Some may not like the U.S. government or its leader, whichever iteration of either, but American culture as a whole is desirable in Germany and much emulated. *Mc* prefix aside, Germans also love to swear in English because its vulgarities often hold the sort of meaning that cannot otherwise be perfectly encapsulated in a single word. Even Chancellor Angela Merkel is fond of casually dropping the stateside word "shitstorm." She may well have used that or some other English profanity when she saw the reports that said President Donald Trump—rather ham-fistedly—tried to get CureVac, a German firm working on a corona-virus vaccine, to move its research wing to the United States, ostensibly to develop said vaccine exclusively for his country. From the level of cultural role model and Marshall Plan economic saviour, the U.S. has seriously declined in its relations with Germany. It didn't help matters when, a little later, the president announced he was going to remove nearly 10,000 of his 34,500 troops in Germany, where the United States has extensive overseas bases. That prompted one German lawmaker to warn that the only winners in such a move would be Russia and China.

So once again, while the United States continued to fritter away its goodwill, China was going around the world handing out face masks, taking advantage of its favourable position. The so-called factory of the world dominates all sorts of supply chains. China is the world's biggest supplier of the raw materials for medication. Before the pandemic, China made one out of every two of the world's face masks. When it was first hit by the virus, being the only one, it also had unfettered access to more of the global supply of protective equipment. When the rest of the world started feeling the effects later, they discovered China had scooped up all the face masks and other gear. Nothing suggests this was malicious, of course. China was dealing with a spectre it had never seen before and legitimately needed the equipment. But the fallout cannot be disputed. Lacking protective gear and life-saving tools, the West and the rest were left more vulnerable, and that scramble for what they lacked caused discord, division, and ultimately, dependency on China. That made China powerful, and China knows it. According to Horizon Advisory, again, the sort of market share and resources China intends to seize amid the pandemic are "especially those that force dependence."

The cost of Western countries' dependence has been made painfully obvious by the pandemic. But the dependence is not just on China. It is also on each other. Nations are reeling as they realize that the pursuit of efficiency, the sourcing of supplies from around the world, has demonstrated their vulnerabilities. So, with the decline of the world order we've known will be another decline—the decline of our interconnectedness that has been its chief pillar. As the world becomes less stable, so too will it become more divided. We were already seeing this before the pandemic; the outbreak of COVID-19 just laid it bare and provided a push.

16

Risako was leaving Germany. Her university in Japan was actually ordering her home. She didn't have a choice, and she was sad. With the travel restrictions, with every country banning everyone but citizens and residents, once Risako went back to Japan, she was uncertain when she would be able to return to Germany and her studies. I'd see Elias again, of course, what with his having family in Canada, but Risako? I don't know. Probably never. That made me sad.

Not long after, I received an email about my own plans for returning home: my flight back to Canada, a prized, nonstop Munich–Toronto route, had been cancelled. The only source of comfort was that they did not require me to call in once more. The airline had automatically issued me a new ticket. It was probably a source of comfort for them as well, not having to listen to my voice yet again. The problem, though, was that the new route was no longer nonstop. It had two connections, first in Frankfurt and then Montreal.

In normal times, I would not have minded a few transfers, but with the pandemic and how fast things could change, any layover added an extra layer of risk. If an onward flight got cancelled, I could very well get stuck mid-route. I had already almost had that happen to me in China. I did not want to dance with the devil yet again. But I did not have a choice.

Travel had effectively become an act of desperation. As countries shut their borders, travellers became trapped in severe lockdowns, sometimes kept unilaterally in their hotel rooms, watching entire airports close, their hopes of returning home turning bleak. People were having to pay through the nose for accommodations—expenses for which they hadn't planned. The more fortunate ones were paying near-business-class prices for specially arranged government repatriation flights. Along with restricting inbound travel, the European Union had also issued a directive to allow foreigners already on the continent to remain beyond the terms of their visas, already anticipating some might get stuck due to the disruptions. The excitement and expectation of travel as most of us had known it had ceased to be—it was now fraught with fear, apprehension, and an uncertain outcome. As I walked to the train station to see Risako off, I couldn't help but think that this simple gesture of saying goodbye to someone was in danger of disappearing too, and perhaps of not returning for some time—a small representation of something bigger.

While the insidious creep of COVID-19 was decimating human travel, it was doing much the same to the free flow of goods, as important supply chains between countries slowed to a halt. Businesses and countries alike are now having to reconsider the globalized manner in which they conduct commerce. Returning to normal after this pandemic has passed may be hugely risky, knowing what we know, hearing what we hear from epidemiologists who had, years ago, predicted something like this would happen and are predicting it will happen again.

U.S. president Donald Trump's trade adviser had used the breakdown of supply chains to argue for more pullback from international commerce, saying his country needed to "bring home its manufacturing capabilities and supply chains for essential medicines." That is an attitude likely to be replicated throughout the world, a lasting residue of the widespread pandemic self-interestedness of countries in obtaining supplies. *Foreign Policy* magazine polled twelve experts from a wide range of fields, eight of whom predicted many countries will turn further inward in some way after the crisis.

That inward-turning will not be just the dispassionate decision of business, nor solely the begrudging, cold cost of saving lives. It will be driven also by feelings, by hatred and fear and by anguish. It will be driven by the wave of anti-Asian COVID-19 racism in the West. It will be driven by the hogwash theories that call the coronavirus a conspiracy by the Jewish or Chinese, or that blame immigrants for overwhelming American healthcare. It will be driven by the rising discrimination in China against foreigners as well. Above all, it will be driven by a certain never-again determination born out of vulnerability. When Germany intercepted face masks bound for Switzerland; when a French firm had to call the British health service to say it could not deliver protective equipment because it had been barred by its government; when an American company said the same to the Canadian government; or when President Trump reportedly tried to lure away the German vaccine-maker CureVac—these events confirmed that while we may not long remember the friendships of summer, we will never forget the frustrations forged in this pandemic winter. Both ethnic and—especially—national lines will only be more starkly drawn, driven by factors both primal and pragmatic. And with globalization so intrinsically and inextricably tied to the international order, so, too, will the drifting apart of nations further strain the way of the world.

Reports of the death of everything, however, are greatly exaggerated. Globalization and the world order are more than the sum of their parts. It's greater than the lust for wander and the curiosity for what lies beyond the river or cliff—and the river or cliff beyond that. It's the ability to satiate those desires under well-defined rules, which ensure that how much players can participate and gain isn't solely determined by their power. We have never perfected, and probably will never perfect, any such system. But this bending toward international engagement and stability is universal and, as such, will not just go away that quickly. More links and deeper ties to the rest of the world have been the way of every international order, from the Mongol Empire to the *Pax Romana* to the United Kingdom's imperialist expansion in a dominion where the proverbial sun never set. With the pandemic, we will surely see decline, but not necessarily destruction—or replacement.

As the U.S. general Douglas MacArthur said about soldiers, so, too, it might be said about international orders: they never die; they just fade away. They take a long time to get replaced. The Roman Empire declined for centuries before it fell. It was not until nearly four hundred years later, under Charles the Great's Holy Roman Empire, that these fragments were melded together again in a way that even slightly resembled the previous whole. In imperial China, the lines of regimes that controlled the whole country were separated by long periods with telling names such as the Three Kingdoms, the Sixteen Kingdoms, and the Five Dynasties and Ten Kingdoms. It's nearly impossible to predict such things, but with the weight of the pandemic upon the chaos of Europe, the shrinking international presence of the United States, the inward-turning of nations, and the opportunism of China and Russia, the world order feels like it's in a period of sustained decline and disintegration until some new era begins, however long it may take for that to happen. Before the Qin Dynasty, the first to unite all of China, the historical period was called the Warring States. That is, of course, not a predestined path. Yet, as the financier George Soros said about the potential breakup of the European Union post-pandemic, it is more than a "theoretical possibility; it may be the tragic reality."

I hauled Risako's two white suitcases for her, up steps that were too small and through a door that was too narrow, onto the train to Frankfurt, from where she would fly back to her home in Japan. With physical distancing measures very much in mind, I didn't know whether to go for a small hug. Would the other passengers call us out for such intimacy? Or would they just silently judge Risako for the rest of her trip? At the same time, such trains are timed precisely. Risako's might stop at the station for only three or five minutes, and we had already been late in boarding. I had to act on instinct. I said a brief "bye" and left Risako on the train, the white suitcases between us, and I did not look back.

PART FIVE
THE GATHERING STORM

17

Risako texted me upon her arrival in Japan. Her country had been testing most incoming travellers for COVID-19, she said. "Still waiting for the result in the airport now. (Someone said it will take more than 8 hours!)"

"Is it painful?" I asked. One testing method was the swabbing of the inside of the mouth, but it wasn't as widely used as the swabbing of the sinus, which isn't pleasant. "I hear they push the stick all the way up your nose." (Actually, the swab goes *through* the nose, almost bisecting the head. Either way, it sounded stinging.)

"Yes, it was a bit painful," Risako twice used an emoji of a face with a single tear. "I thought I gave a small groan."

I gave a small groan myself just reading the message.

Risako eventually tested negative, but she wasn't allowed to leave the airport until that was determined. "I was kept waiting for the result for more than 13 hours!!"

A few days earlier, what had been a recommendation from the Canadian government for people to self-isolate for two weeks upon landing in the country had become mandatory. It was another blow for travel, in the near-term, at least. I didn't think anyone would want to go somewhere if they had to be quarantined for fourteen days when they got there. Japan, though, really upped the ante. I would decidedly not want to go somewhere if, upon arrival, I had a stick shoved through my nose and then had to wait around for half a day to get the result.

That is not to diminish the necessity of testing, of course. Personal comfort is nothing when weighed against collective health. Japan had deployed tests only strategically, for travellers and severe cases, and that seemed to be working. But widespread testing was viewed by experts as an important measure for overcoming the virus. Many countries lacked the equipment. The United States, for example, was at one point testing on a per-capita basis roughly seven hundred times lower than South Korea, even though the two had announced their first cases on the same day. By June of 2020, in terms of per-capita deaths, the United States had outstripped South Korea seventy-to-one. When countries do not test widely, they cannot properly contain COVID-19 because they do not know who has it and thus cannot track how it transmits.

That day, while I texted with Risako, around the globe, coronavirus cases crossed the one-million mark, and they showed no signs of stopping.

To the north of me in Germany, a Bolivian flute orchestra, stuck in the country due to travel restrictions, holed up in Rheinsberg Palace (said to be haunted by the ghost of Frederick the Great), surrounded by twenty-three packs of wolves. To the south, Thailand's sixty-seven-year-old king Maha Vajiralongkorn had allegedly holed up with twenty concubines in the Bavarian mountains in a four-star hotel.

The Thais, of course, weren't particularly happy. As their king hid in the mountains, they lived under a state of emergency. When news of the monarch's latest antics reached home, the phrase, "Why do we need a king?" appeared in Thai 1.2 million times on Twitter within twenty-four hours.

Perhaps he felt it was a small price to pay for what must have been a fantastic alpine adventure. Me, I lived considerably more humbly, my surroundings a little less lavish.

More and more, I spent my time running, with my fifteen-euro supermarket shoes. Around the world, no doubt by default, running had become a popular pandemic activity amid gym closures and the necessary decline of team and contact sports. The fitness-conscious people who normally pursued other activities—like me—all started to make do with running, a solitary and socially distanced sport if ever there was one. On Strava, an app that tracks your run and connects you with other runners, I kept getting alerts about new friends joining. I looked it up to see if Strava was publicly listed and was disappointed I couldn't buy shares.

A former colleague of mine at the *Toronto Star*, Wendy Gillis, an avid runner, wrote about the activity and its relation to the pandemic. "Our worlds have shrunk, and we cannot move as freely through our own city," she wrote. Zipping around on foot, faster than just walking but slower than driving, does enable detailed, intimate observations of your environment while still covering serious ground. "I have never been more grateful for running."

Me too, I came to find. I appreciated my long runs and the sport in general. The weather began to warm, and it allowed me to connect with Bayreuth in the absence of being able to shop, eat, and meet the people there. I didn't enjoy walking the central district, but running outside was different; there was an earthly warmth to it. The empty downtown felt like every empty downtown these days—forbidding and ghost-like, the few inhabitants on the streets and sidewalks all trying to avoid each other as much as possible. Outside the core, though, the concrete and sandstone faded quickly into the wild, into a place that seemed far away from the sick world. I got to know the branches and shrubs of the Studentenwald and the damp mud beneath my feet; the careless cows behind their electric fences; the thickly coated llamas and alpacas, in need of a shave, in the outdoor zoo that had no doors to shut; the gravel crunching under the soles and the sight of horses and the sound of trees. I ran three times a week, ten kilometres at a time. Like my former colleague Wendy did when she trained for a marathon in 2016, I gauged my run only by my watch, turning back when time was up. I didn't have a plan, running wherever I liked, with no direction except forward. It felt good, liberating. Wendy had used escapism-laced language to describe her pandemic exercise. She "fled," she wrote. She "tried to run away from it all." I felt that was most apt.

As the number of those infected piled up and the lockdowns intensi-fied, the stock market, after recording historic crashes at the beginning of the pandemic, actually picked up considerably, riding the waves of government stimulus packages around the world. But it was looking more and more like a hollow rebound. The coming recession was still on track to be worse than that of the 2008 financial crisis, according to multiple investment banks. Morgan Stanley said U.S. growth would slow to a "74-year low."

Government stimulus was largely how the world climbed out of the slump caused in 2008, which at its heart was a storm caused by those in the world of finance, the collapse of complicated investment instruments, losses of ones and zeros and money on paper that rippled outward. Thus, in 2008, we saw government bailouts, interest-rate cuts, and quantitative easing measures rolled out—financial means to solve a financial problem. For a crisis like this, with more tangible factors, the trillions in stimulus that governments have already injected and the likely trillions more to come only treats the symptoms. "The best that economic and financial policymakers can do . . . is limit the damage," the German insurer Allianz's top economist said in the media. "They cannot turn the economy around because this is a health issue, not an economic or financial issue." And you cannot print more hospitals like money or cut the spread rate of a virus through a parliamentary vote.

That same logic, unfortunately, can be applied to everything that has stemmed from the spread of the virus, such as the shake-up of the world order or the divisions it has caused—when we tackle those problems, we do not address the core issue. That applies even to the virus itself. We can develop coronavirus resistance, the so-called herd immunity, if enough people get infected and enough die. We can develop vaccines and overcome the months, if not years, of trials and the logistical nightmare of distribution. And in the meantime, we can isolate the infected, prevent mass interactions, wash our hands, and hide our faces. But for all that, most of the infected, those whose symptoms are not life-threatening, are just told to stay home and take painkillers.

Using ventilators or drugs on those writhing and clawing for breath can only treat their symptoms, not help to find a lasting cure. And all we can do as a society is the same thing that any one of those patients can do: prolong the fight and wait and pray for the immune system to conjure up its magic to kill the enemy. Just as economic measures do not address the public health issue at the heart of the crisis, our public health measures themselves do little to combat the underlying pathological threat.

In that same vein, even conquering the pathological threat, as will only occur when we find a vaccine, will not address the deeper underlying issue: the world has been caught unprepared by an epic crisis that has made grand spectacle of our inherent blind spots and narrow vision, our helplessness against the vast spectre of the unknown, and our repeated cycles of ill-preparedness and blame-laying when faced with calamity. The pandemic has revealed faults and fault lines far older than itself. It is demonstrating, uncomfortably, that ill-preparedness may be inevitable. The pandemic is a warning, its message distilled in the fact that, for COVID-19, just like during the Black Death, like the clergy with their healing ceremonies and the so-called doctors with their funny beak-shaped masks, we too had no cure.

18

The United Kingdom performed a pandemic simulation in 2016 that, among other findings, revealed the country's incapacity to deal with an outbreak should one arise. Naturally, the government later came under fire for not following up on its own recommendations from that exercise. In 2018, U.S. president Donald Trump's administration dismantled a unit in the White House responsible for preparing for pandemics. In 2019, the U.S. Department of Health ran a months-long simulation of a respiratory virus that spread from China and, in so doing, predicted inadequate physical distancing but plenty of in-fighting among both federal departments and states. The U.S. Federal Emergency Management Agency had warned of pandemic vulnerability months before the pandemic. U.K. prime minister Boris Johnson boasted about shaking hands "with everybody" at a hospital before he himself got diagnosed with COVID-19 and spent forty-eight hours in intensive care, where "things could have gone either way." Examples such as these are more plentiful than not. In the lead-up to the current crisis, it seemed the world, and its leaders especially, had done everything that wasn't supposed to be done.

Such obstinance in the face of fact and warning does not, obviously, just apply to pandemics. There was an entire commission established to find out how U.S. intelligence and security forces got blindsided on September 11, 2001. George Tenet, the director of the Central Intelligence Agency, who had heard whispers of a potential attack, had stormed into National Security Adviser Condoleezza Rice's office with news of an imminent extremist threat. Rice later wrote she did not recall that direct warning from the CIA chief "because we were discussing the threat every day." Not a specific threat, but the general, spectral idea of an attack on American soil, someday soon. With increasing complexity, our world has become one of a multitude of looming disasters and impending catastrophes, each coming with the direst warnings from the most wizened of experts, arguing passionately for their cause. Yet each prediction also remains unpredictable in its precise timing or how exactly it might escalate. And to be fair, conjuring up a scenario whereby two commercial airplanes are commandeered by box-cutting suicidal hijackers and flown into the World Trade Center, or of a virus originating from a bat in a Chinese wet market that would force a lockdown of the entire world, is not necessarily a skill most of us possess, especially our leaders, unfortunately. It's more in the realm of Quentin Tarantino and fanciful screenwriters like Scott Z. Burns, who wrote the 2011 thriller *Contagion*, which rather presciently chronicles a virus originating from a bat.

We are fundamentally bad at gauging threats. Research shows we view danger not with our calculated, higher-order thinking, but with the base and instinctual hunches formed through eons. Brain scans even show that we subconsciously think of our future selves as different people. We expect our leaders to be more disciplined—Condoleezza Rice is hardly a slouch in the brains department—but it's easy to say in hindsight what could have been done. Five years ago, what politician would have prioritized stocking up on ventilators over tackling climate change or proposing gun regulations or addressing any of the other problems of the day that could just as easily have escalated? Taken individually, just about every crisis could have been averted, yet these unexpected blows will keep coming, for we are simply incapable of complete prevention. We were designed for threats up-close and carnivorous, the short-faced bear in the tall grass and the sabre-toothed Smilodon stalking the plains, not the abstract dooms hovering above, compounding and waiting for a spark.

The late U.K. prime minister Margaret Thatcher said Europe had averted wars for decades because of the deterrent effect of nuclear weapons. That brings to mind the joke about elephant repellant, a purple powder sprayed all around by a man who says the absence of those big mammals is evidence of the dust's effectiveness. Maybe in a world without nuclear weapons, Europe would have headed toward apocalypse and annihilation. But we can never truly prove that as a fact. There is no way to definitively know which catastrophe has been averted and which has not through whatever we have done. Imagine the countless crises that have been avoided all the times our leaders have had the necessary foresight and done the right thing. We do not know about and cannot point to any such examples because the very essence of their being is in being unknown. None of us ever experienced them.

There is thus no such thing as a crisis of this scale for which we were prepared; a crisis is inherently an event for which we were unprepared. If we had been prepared for the pandemic, if we had done everything right and lost no lives, then it would not have been a pandemic but rather a vaguely worrisome little blip that barely registered in our consciousness. Maybe for decades, that was precisely what happened: all the safeguards were in place, and all this time we've been constantly saved without knowing it. Politicians would have looked at that costly health spending and said: "What do we need all this for, when there are no pandemics to deal with?" "Why bother with the recommendations from this silly simulation?" "Why buy ventilators?" And proponents might have argued, "There are no pandemics precisely because it's been working!"—maybe and probably true, but mostly, if not completely, unprovable. Many experts may have foreseen a looming pandemic, but who could have known it would be this specific bat-borne bane from Wuhan in December 2019? Even they, the people sounding the drums back then, could not have beaten their booms with the same gusto as they did after the fact. When the experts made their case against cutting funding, even they would have understood at least a small part of what the politicians heard—the elephant joke. Maybe the fact that we had been prepared for years is precisely the reason we are unprepared now, a cycle doomed to repeat.

In the animated television comedy *Family Guy*, when staring down the barrel of a gun, Mayor Adam West says, "I have a tiny bulletproof shield the exact size of a bullet somewhere on my body." If West were to be hit in that spot, he says, he would be unharmed: "You'll be the laughingstock of me." The physics, of course, doesn't make sense. The entire point of a Kevlar vest is that it spreads the projectile's impact over a wide area so it does not penetrate the skin. A shield the size of a bullet simply does not work. But let's assume it does. The other, more obvious problem still remains: West does not and cannot know where the shooter's bullet will strike. No matter how hard we try, how masterfully we attempt to plot the path of disaster, predicting for just a single circumstance is impossible. In the Second World War, the British expected a naval assault on Singapore and armed the south with canons pointed to the sea. The Japanese came from the other side, through the Malaysian jungles, on bicycles. If only those big British guns were in the north. In the wake of the North Sea flood of 1953, the Dutch built the mightiest dyke system ever, only for the next destructive, overwhelming tide to come from the inland waterways. If only they had built the dam around the rivers, then all that death and destruction could have been avoided. If only we had just stocked up on the ventilators and test kits the pandemic world so desperately needs, then far fewer people might have died. But it doesn't work that way.

Experts aside, many critics came to realize the importance of ventilators precisely because so many died. Then they may say we need to make note of what was not done this time and start doing it. But consider what would happen if the next crisis is just slightly different in where it begins or how it afflicts people or spreads. In a way, that is precisely what happened with COVID-19. Everything else aside, one reason U.S. health authorities did not have enough test kits was because they had reportedly been anticipating a different type of pandemic—not coronavirus, but influenza, like the 2009 swine flu, which required completely different test kits. Those were the very experts sounding the drums, and to be fair to them, an influenza pandemic could just as easily have been the case.

It is perhaps impossible to predict the specific pathway of the next big threat—or even to pin down its broad nature, as argued by the former U.S. general Stanley McChrystal in his book on interconnectedness and complexity, *Team of Teams*. Imagine coloured billiard balls, arranged in a triangle, being struck by the white cue ball. The onward motion of the coloured spheres is based on how they are hit, but they also hit each other and bounce on the edges of the table. Then maybe they bounce against each other again. In that system, any small deviation in any component—the motion of the white ball, the flatness of the table, the smoothness of the felt—ripples massively and unpredictably. The term "butterfly effect" comes from the academic paper, "Does the Flap of a Butterfly's Wings in Brazil Set Off a Tornado in Texas?" in which a researcher recounts how a rounding error caused a massive divergence of data in his complex weather-forecasting model. Our densely integrated world has become like that weather model—or those tightly packed billiard balls. This is a world in which events that may previously have been isolated now ripple farther and wider—and in ways we do not expect and can hardly foresee.

We cannot be prepared for every eventuality, and it is the ones for which we are unprepared that will devastate. Every property of COVID-19 hits at our raw, exposed nerves. It spreads through the air, and we have a complex web of international travel. It is mild enough to be passed by unsuspecting carriers, and we live in densely packed cities. It causes breathing difficulties, and we lack ventilators. But there was no brilliant mind that tailored this plague just for us. Nature is just a cesspool of disease, constantly flinging a wide assortment of filth. Humanity has been a successful animal and has no doubt fought off countless extinction-level threats, some without us even knowing it, as the lesser viruses that failed to target our weaknesses died in oblivion. We see only the few plagues that snaked past our armour and pierced our softest spot beneath. Thus the path of the pestilence is a bit like how lighting arches across the sky. Even with the massive electrical resistance of the air, the bolt finds a way. And its specific path—narrow, winding, and unpredictable—is paved precisely because of that resistance and not in spite of it.

There is a lesson to be learned from the pandemic, but that lesson is not, as the saying goes, to emulate the generals who are always fighting the last war. The lesson is that the threat we do not see will have the most impact, and that we do not know what we cannot know. In *The Black Swan*, Nassim Nicholas Taleb writes: "Consider a turkey that is fed every day. Every single feeding will firm up the bird's belief that it's the general rule of life to be fed every day by a friendly member of the human race." Then, just before Thanksgiving, the same hand that feeds the turkey brings a blade to its neck. Nothing a turkey does in its life, nothing it ever learns, and no amount of cunning or diligence on the part of the bird can ever prepare it for its day of slaughter. To be truly ready for the next crisis, we have to accept the humbleness of the human set against the ceaseless cruelty of the cosmos, that there will always be a calamity for which we are ill-prepared.

19

A possible ancestor of mine is the Chinese emperor Yu the Great, from the third millennium B.C.E. The keyword, however, is "possible." My father told me about this potential connection after some Internet research, and years later, he would in fact deny ever saying it at all. I'd always found the link dubious anyway, like how Egyptian Ptolemaic kings claimed descent from gods and legend. The other possibility, my father said in the conversation he does not remember, was that we descended from nameless nomadic Mongols, which is far more believable. Yu, after all, came from an era in Chinese history during which records weren't well kept, so history is often mixed in myth. But veracity aside, Yu's story is relevant, emerging out of an era of havoc wreaked on China by great floods, only ended, finally, by Yu himself. For while others had attempted and failed to tame the tides by setting up barriers to block the flow of the water, Yu succeeded by drawing irrigation canals, diverting and splitting the waterways.

Nearly four thousand years later, Dutch engineers would have the same idea. It came to them fresh after terrible floods in the 1990s, when the Meuse, Rhine, and Waal rivers swelled with mountain melt-water and flooded in a way their earlier billion-dollar wall-against-the-sea could never have prevented. So, the Netherlands government tried something new, as Stanley McChrystal notes in *Team of Teams*. It had to fortify the rivers, and to do so, it started carving out new water-ways. In some places, instead of building higher dykes to guard against rising water, engineers lowered them, so that farmland around could serve as floodplains. The people already living there were relocated. The plan was called "Room for the River." The Dutch and Yu had accepted a fundamental rethinking in how to tackle the tides: that the reality of floods is inevitable. They did not focus on trying to control the course of the current. They sought instead the ability to deal with it. The essence of this idea is encapsulated in a quote often attributed to Greek mythology, when Atlas, forced by Zeus to hold up the world, pleads not for the erasure of the punishment but for the ability to take on the task: "I do not pray for a lighter load, but for a stronger back."

There will be another pandemic, a catastrophic natural disaster, a major war, a great recession, a tumultuous upheaval, or an unprece-dentedly new crisis that will catch the world off-guard, like the turkey and the blade to its neck. If we cannot prevent the universe from crash-ing upon us when least expected, bearing down with all the weight of the epochs, and if we cannot predict the specific nature of the threat, then we can hope only for resiliency in the face of that. We, similarly, need to strengthen our backs.

While nobody was truly ready for the pandemic, some countries acted fast and decisively, and that saved lives, one study showed: At its peak,

South Korea had 0.1 deaths per million residents per day, while the figures for Germany and Denmark were about the same at 2.8 deaths. It's a big range, but despite that, those figures are all considered to be on the low end of the spectrum. Sweden, which believed in a different method and did not enforce lockdowns for its citizens, and Italy, which acted late, had more than 10 deaths per million people per day. Spain had nearly 20 per million. Research suggests that if the United States had locked down just one week earlier, it could have avoided more than 35,000 deaths. If it were two weeks, 50,000 deaths. The top qualities we need in the face of any crisis are nimbleness and resiliency. The greatest failure of many countries against the pandemic wasn't the failure to predict and prepare, it was the failure to react. Leery of stepping on individual liberties, much of the West had suffered from that. However suddenly the lockdowns came later, they were all too late. The world needs to do better.

Such a conversation, of course, cannot be had without the prime yet complicated example of China, where the virus originated but where the government response was quick and decisive, not to mention effective, at least in the short term. Already known for keeping close tabs on its citizenry, the Chinese government went into hyperdrive during the worst days of the pandemic, tracking mobile phones through ubiquitous apps and compliant telco companies and unprecedentedly locking down entire cities and even regions of the country. The Communist Party's more than 90 million members became lockdown enforcers. There were stories of violators being tied to poles or otherwise humiliated publicly and coercively quarantined. Two medical facilities, 2,600 beds in total, were built in ten days. Then, as the Western world reeled,

Chinese hospitals that were once overwhelmed had unoccupied beds. Drug trials had difficulty enrolling volunteers as new infections dropped. That bliss was disturbed just two months later when a relaxation of lockdown rules brought a new wave of infection, which just goes to show how effective everything had all been. The Chinese authoritarianism at the heart of the response was cited as a shining example of how to handle the outbreak. A *Bloomberg* headline about the initial draconian lockdown on Hubei read, "China Sacrifices a Province to Save the World from Coronavirus." China's "bold approach" was "ambitious, agile, and aggressive," and it had worked, read a World Health Organization report. That's one way to look at it, but China being China, things are never one dimensional — its reaction to the virus is hardly one to emulate — quite the opposite given other, darker, aspects of its approach.

The central government certainly reacted quickly to the outbreak, but between the first reported cases and the January 23 lockdown, the virus had stirred in Wuhan for nearly a month. The first reactions of local officials to the virus had been to cover it up. Heads roll easily in China — literally. From Chongqing to Hangzhou and Suzhou, from judicial chiefs to vice mayors, many have faced the death penalty for a plethora of crimes. In the aftermath of crises, such as the SARS epidemic, floods, and earthquakes, local officials are routinely suspended, dismissed, demoted, or blacklisted. Perhaps Western leaders can learn a lesson in accountability from China's post-crises retributions, although when you're dealing with a country where rule of law is questionable, where those purged can rarely dream of a fair and open trial, it is not surprising local officials responded to the pandemic by hauling to the interrogation room the whistleblower, Dr. Li Wenliang, who later died of the virus. Local bureaucrats valued their image and their careers more than containment and feared the wrath of their bosses more than the devastation of the plague, and that cost the world dearly.

However much China's subsequent swift clampdown stunted the spread of the virus, that same effort spent earlier would have had a drastically bigger impact. With one carrier transmitting to several others, infections grow exponentially, meaning the virus spreads more quickly the longer it gets to spread. If it's not stifled in the seed, it takes vastly more effort to try to contain it later on. According to research from the University of Southampton in the United Kingdom, China could have prevented 95 per cent of infections if it had acted quickly from the first hint of trouble. That delay may have been fuelled by different factors than the slow reactions of Italy, Spain, or the United States, but its impact was the same. Nimbleness, or the lack of it, has less to do with forms of government that it may appear.

Indeed, the countries that have been able to get by, with relatively low infection or death rates, are varied and, in some ways, fundamentally different from each other. There are those like South Korea and Singapore, which did move with more authority than others, with aggressive testing and contact-tracing that invited privacy concerns. Singapore did end up with a second wave of infections from its sometimes-overlooked migrant-worker population, and each successful country has its own faults. But for the most part, they showed a certain level of success, and they all shared something. They were able to move quickly because, on the whole, their people voluntarily accepted the trade-off of certain liberties in exchange for the common good.

A good case study is New Zealand's response, widely cited by experts as successful, and with a noted absence of criticism from human rights groups. The country restricted travel early, prior even to any known cases, and started widely testing and contact-tracing. Eventually, there was an initial spike of cases in the country, like everywhere, but in the phrasing of the health-policy mantra going around at the time, that curve was quickly flattened. In April of 2020, New Zealand's cases stabilized in the 1,100-range, with under ten new instances of infection per day. By May, only twenty were dead, and soon after, the authorities there started reporting zero new cases. New Zealand definitely has natural advantages, being a sparsely populated collection of islands with only five million people. But the success of the country's pandemic response, the reason it had been able to act so quickly, draws from a deeper reserve. Mid-pandemic, a poll showed nearly nine in ten New Zealanders trusted their government to make the right decisions about COVID-19, compared to the average of six in ten in G7 countries. New Zealand's numbers were not just the result of people's gravitation toward bigger government amid crisis. The country has always had high levels of public trust, which had been rising over the years. In 2018, when citizens were asked whether they trusted the State to do what is right, 65 per cent said yes, compared with 48 per cent in 2016. So, in 2019, when a mass shooter killed fifty people, Prime Minister Jacinda Ardern was able to announce an assault-rifle ban within a week, which became law within a month. Regardless of whether that ban was warranted, it demonstrated an ability to act quickly and with the backing of public trust. What made New Zealanders comply with the government's orders to stay home wasn't the heavy enforcement of

China, but the same belief held by the Germans, the South Koreans, and all the other countries that were able to respond relatively quickly, that the government was doing or, at least, trying to do the right thing. Therein lies the key to nimbleness—a wellspring of public faith, usually built up over years. As obvious as it is when it's there, it's glaring when it's not.

Enter the United States, where confidence in public institutions isn't even held by its current president, who makes a habit of raging about the supposed entrenched, unelected "Deep State" that is constantly out to get him. In 2019, the U.S. citizenry's trust in the government was a pitiful 17 per cent, so it wasn't exactly a surprise that protests broke out against the lockdowns and restrictions. In a country long steeped in its constitution's protection of individual freedoms, a belief often taken to the extreme, the demonstrations ranged from a few hundred protestors to several thousands and slammed the financial and social impacts of the containment measures, demanding they be reversed. In the state of Michigan, protestors—armed with both guns and the Second Amendment that protected their right to do so— stormed the state legislature building. Lawmakers wore bullet-proof vests. Then they cancelled a scheduled session to avoid armed confrontation. And in the state of New Hampshire, whose motto emphasizes liberty above all, similar protests occurred in front of the legislature, prompting Canada's the *Beaverton* humour website to write this headline: "Protestor holding up 'Live Free or Die' sign excited to do both."

When the people and their government are so far apart, it is a hard if not impossible task to introduce something as drastic as a nationwide lockdown. Politicians, under pressure to bend to popular whims instead of expert advice, may think more about their job security than what's best for the public. Action becomes delayed and lethargic, and any enforcement is made difficult by the public's lack of faith in those trying to impose the law. The numbers speak for themselves: In April of 2020, with more than twenty thousand deaths, the United States surpassed Italy as the country with the highest COVID-19 mortality. Even if adjusted for population, by June the United States still had the ninth-highest deaths per million people at 366.3. New Zealand had just 4.6 deaths per million.

Jean-Yves Duclos, a Canadian cabinet minister who serves as the vice-chair of the country's official coronavirus committee, has said that, to tackle the pandemic, the government needs to "think in a different mode." Words to live by, not just for whatever next pandemic hits our shores but in responding to other crises as well. But it's not so much "a different mode" as a fundamental realignment of our preparedness that is needed, with a particular accent on agility. And if what we've learned is that public trust and open, transparent government lies at the heart of that agility, then more than anything, the pandemic has been a wakeup call to build better societies.

And as public trust in our governments needs to improve, so too does our collective trust in the international bodies that were set up to deal with such challenges as those posed by the pandemic. Certain issues are just too big to tackle alone, or they involve a direct need for speed that cannot tolerate duplications of effort. The search for the COVID-19 vaccine is one of them. The virus, after all, knows no borders, and neither may the next crisis. What started as a China problem quickly morphed into everyone's problem, not unlike how war in the Middle East creates refugees that destabilize Europe, how coal emissions in a developing country heat up the atmosphere for all of us. More and more, with COVID-19 acting as a clear and sharp exclamation point, it is becoming evident that our best defence in handling such crises is working together and doing so quickly and efficiently.

But, of course, it is easy to say that. "We did not score enough points this time and need to try harder next time to score more points, while making sure the opposing players score fewer points," says the losing team's captain in every post-game interview in every single sport. The way countries reacted to the pandemic was, generally, an extension of how those societies were shaped, a reflection of their cultures and socio-political situations. Nimbleness and flexibility are built over decades, if not centuries. Particularly, with the pandemic's having torn at the heart of the world, leaving future resiliency in question, the solution is not a simple matter of just being better. Rather, it is committing to the kind of broader infrastructure that makes countries more cohesive, trusting of their leaders, and ultimately prepared for whatever the cosmos throws at them. That should be obvious, especially in the wake of COVID-19. What is less obvious is the road there.

2 0

The end of April marked a new day in Bayreuth. I had been in Germany so long that the stores had begun to open again. In the state of Bavaria, the government announced that restaurants were unfortunately still closed for dining in, but nonessential businesses with floor spaces of under eight hundred square metres were allowed to open, albeit with a new rule: you had to wear face masks when entering. Dutifully, I put on my uncle's Honeywell for the first time in more than a month, the first time since China, and I made for the Euroshop discount chain that had the one-euro wines Elias had mentioned. I was handed a shopping basket at the door, for everyone had to have one, which was a new rule of sorts. That way, with a limited number of baskets, the shop controlled the number of people who could be on the premises at any time. I forget how many baskets it was, but it wasn't a lot, no more than a half-dozen. I had to wait for one shopper to finish paying before entering. I found the system quite clever, but what I did not find was one-euro wine. Either they were sold out or it was only Elias's wishful thinking.

Exempted from Bavaria's announced eight-hundred-square-metre rule were bookstores, which I thought was interesting. As lockdowns were eased, what governments allowed to open first often showed their priorities and those of their societies in general. Not to cast aspersions on Canada, but Ontario's provincial government allowed housekeepers, nannies, and cooks to return to work and opened marinas and golf courses while still discouraging interactions from people in different households. "I'd like to personally congratulate rich people," wrote one journalist. "Ontario: where your butler can come over, but not your mother," said another.

Just three days after bookstores were allowed to open in Bayreuth and environs, Albert Camus's classic *The Plague* started leaping off the shelves, climbing to the top of bestseller lists. *The Plague* depicts a fictional pestilence in the 1940s, but it remains ever-relevant because it is really about authoritarian power—"only when a strong wind was blowing did a faint, sickly odour coming from the east remind them that they were living under a new order." It isn't so much about the pathological plague as it is about the human and societal condition. Camus writes about hope and heroism, but also says the plague "never dies or disappears for good." If and when the plague returns, Camus writes, when it "would rouse up its rats again," the world will not have emerged stronger and more resilient, and that resurgence will be "for the bane and the enlightening of men." Plague theme aside, it doesn't take a lot of thought to see why Germans would make this book a bestseller almost seventy-five years after it was first published.

———

In the *Harry Potter* series, abusively repressing a young wizard's abilities generates an "obscurus," a floating mass of destructive energy. It's the chief plot line of the *Fantastic Beasts* spinoff movies, in fact. But it's not an entirely new idea. In a 2005 *X-Men* comic-book story arc, swaths of superpowered mutants losing their abilities results in a similar mass of energy dubbed "the Collective." The idea that trauma does not just go one-way into a black hole, that its effect compounds, bound to echo destructively, is universal and constant. Moreover, energy cannot be destroyed, whether it's that of magic being suppressed or mutant abilities erased—or the vigour and restlessness of ordinary humans kept indoors with nothing to do. That demands an outlet. One study estimated COVID-19 could lead to 75,000 "deaths of despair" in the United States from suicide and drug and alcohol abuse. Across North America, gun sales have spiked. The Federal Bureau of Investigation performed 3.7 million related background checks in one month, the most since the current gun-regulation system was introduced in 1998. And these figures represent only the effects we are able to see and quantify, mere momentary manifestations of a poison more enduring, one tiny corner of that mass of energy hanging over us.

While I don't think any of my friends have begun to arm to themselves, what I have noted since the pandemic began is a rapid polarization of views in some circles. With the lockdown and the issue of compliance, individual freedom versus collective welfare has become a new line of stark division. At first, I noticed only those who had swung toward hyper-adherence, who cut off all physical contact and stopped seeing their parents, even when the law of the land did not require them to do so. Then there were the libertarian types, the ones who went to secret gyms and barbers and speakeasies that defied closure orders, who wined with friends in the park and then heatedly debated with the police breaking up the party. There are also the conspiracy theorists. One Facebook friend started believing everything was a hoax by the establishment to try to control people's lives, and he did not stop there. I started seeing an increase of posts from him about world-wide child-trafficking conspiracies and a shadowy network of celeb-rities, banking families, and the American Left. He was not like that before COVID-19, at least not outwardly. Sometimes, I think about him and wonder if I should have said something, questioned his reasoning, or perhaps asked him if he was really okay. I mean, if ever there was a time for closeted conspiracy theorists to come out, it's now. COVID-19 is almost perfectly built for such things—science fiction and images of a dystopian world made real. Was this all a global government plot to subjugate us and take away our freedoms and even our lives? Most likely not. But trapped in isolation, left to one's own devices, pinned to social media in a world seemingly collapsing all around you—that's the environment for far-fetched and unhinged thinking, even from those not usually prone to such states of mind.

All things considered, perhaps we shouldn't be surprised that the police killing of an unarmed black man, George Floyd, in the United States sparked mass protests in May 2020—the largest such uprisings since the 1960s. Frustration and anxiety caused by the lockdowns, along with a disproportional pandemic impact on minorities—both health-wise and financially—and an already incendiary situation based on years of heavy-handed policing set off a spark that blew the whole situation sky high. It really did feel like the end of the world—plague, death, race war, and the decline of the international order. Still, I think to be overly pessimistic is missing the point.

The antiracism protestors are not unlike the protestors of Hong Kong, rising against what they see as injustice, trying to effect systemic change. In the context of stability and unity, the world may be strengthened by such protests. In the wake of the pandemic, society may be soundly shaken and trend toward disarray and despondence, but no future is inescapable. Even in the pit of chaos, there remains a choice in how the world may climb from it, to build the sort of resiliency that will help it better take on the next crisis.

The pandemic-driven shift in collective sentiment toward a greater role for the State is an opportunity. Governments would be wise to capitalize on it, not to seize more power or prolong reign but to fortify public faith, listen and act on their people's frustrations, and to prove their leaders are worthy. Governments also need to instill unity so that people may be influenced to value the group over self. Then, if governments issue another lockdown order or whatever novel emergency rule for this or any other crisis, a justifiable measure for collective welfare, they can secure the necessary compliance, even in a free, inherently individualistic society. If nimbleness and resiliency are the top qualities needed in crisis, then every government needs to make fostering public trust and cohesion its primary goal. One can hardly not think of the global challenge of climate change—are there lessons we can learn from this pandemic and how we responded to it, individually and collectively, that may serve us better in that regard?

Of course, not every country will think in that direction; in fact, it's a safe bet most will not, which makes developing a stable and trustworthy international order all the more important. The purpose of such an order would be not just to mount an effective collective crisis response the next time disaster strikes, but to help developing countries build their infrastructure and overall resiliency in the meantime.

In the wake of the plague, with the weakening of the world order only exacerbated, there will no doubt be a thick quagmire to navigate. For long, the liberal international order and those who stand behind it have been, perhaps, naïve. They assumed countries like China and Russia could become, in their view, enlightened like them, ultimately converted to their cause. But geopolitical competition has only intensified. U.S. secretary of state Mike Pompeo may have hoped Hong Kong "would provide a model for authoritarian China," but the opposite has happened. Post-pandemic, as challengers rise, as the system and institutions everyone had taken for granted weaken, how can the world ensure its agility and unity in the face of the next crisis?

I, of course, don't have that answer. I don't think anyone does. But perhaps a change of mindset is in order. Like Yu and the Dutch and their acknowledgement of the inevitability of floodwaters, like how the world needs to realize it will always be caught unprepared by the next crisis, the West needs to accept the decline of its hegemony. Instead of actively trying to stunt the rise of China and Russia, the United States and Europe need to put pressure on them to rise more constructively and, perhaps, share the mantle of global leadership. Hostility and aggression need to be met proportionately, but if the ambitious and hardworking want to grow and prosper, then perhaps the most American thing to do is to let them. Just as challengers to the world order no doubt know that open confrontation helps no one, the West must realize the necessity of co-existence. That's not entirely a new idea. But given how easily one's problem becomes everyone else's in this globalized world, the pandemic has made it all the more important to grasp that oft-repeated truth: to face the next crisis, all need to learn the value of stability and cohesion.

In June of 2020, Singapore's prime minister Lee Hsien Loong wrote in *Foreign Affairs* magazine for the first time. It was twenty-six years after his father, Singapore's founding prime minister Lee Kuan Yew, had appeared in the magazine's pages in a far-ranging interview in which the now-CNN host Fareed Zakaria asked whether China's rise would destabilize the region, and he responded, "I don't think we can speak in terms of just the East Asian order." The late Lee the elder—who spoke like an old-timey movie character, once called the "finest Englishman east of Suez" by the U.K. foreign secretary—had long been a sort of oracle of the Orient, with lines of U.S. presidents and other world leaders regularly soliciting his views. There is thus a historical heft in the essay of Lee the younger, which addressed the China–U.S. geopolitical competition, the international order, and the pandemic:

> Even with the best relations between the United States and China, mounting a collective response to COVID-19 would be hugely challenging. Unfortunately, the pandemic is exacerbating the U.S.–Chinese rivalry, increasing mistrust, one-upmanship, and mutual blame. This will surely worsen if, as now seems inevitable, the pandemic becomes a major issue in the U.S. presidential election.

Lee's words are a warning for the powers and a plea: get your act together; a world mired in a new Cold War will not endure a crisis like this. Countries such as Singapore depend on trade and, thus, stability. Lee has drubbed that drum aplenty. But it is rare for Lee to write an opinion piece, and his choice of publication—a premier can write anywhere—speaks volumes. A top U.S. diplomat has said, "Virtually everyone I know in the foreign-policy-national-security area of the government is attentive to [*Foreign Affairs*]." Lee didn't just want to be heard. He wanted his four thousand words to be heard by the right people. The son of the seer is worried.

Perhaps the best and most accurate answer to how COVID-19 will shape the world comes from the late Chinese leader Zhou Enlai in 1971. He actually misspoke for he had misunderstood the question. But still, the premier's words have become legendary, emblematic of the far-sightedness of an ambitious country. Henry Kissinger, then the U.S. national security adviser, had asked Zhou to assess the impact of the eighteenth-century French Revolution, and the premier responded, "It is too early to tell."

21

From Bayreuth by train, I was to arrive in Nuremberg at 7:57 a.m. on platform 18, and then leave for Munich at 8:02 a.m. from platform 9. I was a little worried about making the connection, given how little breathing room I had afforded myself between trains. I didn't notice that until after I had bought the ticket, probably due to itinerary fatigue, having lost count of how many hours I'd spent booking and rebooking tickets over the course of this trip. Moreover, after arriving at Munich Central Station, I still had to transfer again to get to the airport. I would arrive there with only an hour to spare before my departure. My itinerary was a tightly wound clock, with little redundancy. Any small mishap would effectively throw everything into disarray. The ticket, however, was not refundable or exchangeable, so I didn't have much choice. I've taken bigger risks for less than 45.90 euros, I thought. And if Deutsche Bahn thinks five minutes is a reasonable window to find my way across nine platforms, who am I to argue otherwise?

The problem was I didn't even make it to Nuremberg. In Bayreuth, I waited and waited at the station, but my train never came. I still cannot fathom how this happened, and I've accepted that it will be one of the great mysteries of my life, remaining forever unsolved, like why sandwich meat is round and bread square or why we crown a Miss Universe when all the contestants are from Earth—but it did happen. Whatever was written on my ticket, the time and platform at which the train was supposed to arrive, was simply not true. No train came, and I sat there getting increasingly frustrated. The ticket office at the train station, of course, was closed due to the pandemic. The only staff around was a janitor who told me I had to wear a face mask even on the platform. Like Singapore's airports, I feel German train stations also encapsulate two prominent perceptions of the country: everything runs like clockwork, with connections tightly timed; but then once in a while, you get bureaucratic mishap, and there is no one to approach but an unyielding faceless abyss.

One option was to go back to Elias's apartment to regroup. But I had cleaned the place, packed everything up, and was mentally already in flight. So I decided to take my chances, albeit slim, and go to the airport nonetheless. The next train, if it did come as scheduled, would enable me to arrive at the airport literally in the last few minutes of boarding. It just might be okay. I've made many flights by arriving just on time, with no buffer; and with the pandemic, I wasn't expecting any queues at the gate. I thought there was a more-than-50-per-cent chance I would still make it, and that was enough for me. I spent an additional 70.90 euros on a new ticket at the self-service machine, which I later regretted because, again due to the pandemic, there was no one around to actually check the tickets—I could have ridden free of charge, which I felt I was somehow owed because of the debacle involving the first train. That said, at least this train did show up, and on time, so off I went.

The tightly wound clock became even more tightly wound, and little redundancy became zero redundancy. In keeping with my luck with travel lately, it turned out that the Munich train station was not intuitively designed. I had to transfer from train to subway to get to the airport, and platform 1, where I was supposed to go, was nowhere near where one would expect it to be, at the end of the line of platforms arranged in declining order. It was on the other side, underground. It was a lot of wasted time and long walks, made all the more torturous by the fell weight of twenty-four jars of *schweinskopfsülze* in my luggage. I arrived at the airport check-in counter precisely fifteen minutes after takeoff. Staff at the counter, seemingly unsympathetic to my plight, referred me to another counter, which referred to my mileage program, whose phone lines, running on North America's times, were not yet open.

I eventually did get everything sorted out, but the new flight was the next day, and I was already in Munich and had potentially nowhere to spend the night since, under pandemic rules, hotels only admitted guests under special circumstances. I probably would have qualified for an exception, but figured it just wasn't worth the trouble. For a moment I thought I just might call Thailand's king Maha Vajiralongkorn and his twenty concubines and see if they had a spare bedroom.

I could, of course, have turned around and gone back to where I came from. It wasn't that long a train ride to Bayreuth, only about three hours. It was noon in Germany, and I could still make it back to Elias's apartment to sleep the night and then come back to the airport the next day. With the lack of conductors, I could probably do it for free anyway. But the thought of hauling the twenty-four jars of *schweinskopfsülze* to and fro — not to mention the potential unpredictability of the trains the next morning — was most unappealing. That night, in a largely empty Munich airport, I had some sushi and a Bayreuther Hell beer from the airport supermarket before engaging in a nice chat with a policeman carrying an assault rifle. And there I slept, my last night away from home. In *The Plague*, Albert Camus had written about "travellers caught by the plague and forced to stay where they were," in particular, a journalist stuck in the locked-down town, "the most exiled."

The next day, at the airline counter weigh-in, it dawned on me my haul of *schweinskopfsülze* was pushing the suitcase to thirty kilograms, over the allowed baggage weight. In Thailand, I once used my hand to subtly and slightly — and successfully — lift my luggage while it was weighed to make it appear less heavy. At the Munich counter, I thought about how I should have done that again, and now, how many jars of the meat jelly I would have to eat to reduce the weight. But that was all unnecessary. Amid the layoffs and the lack of human traffic in the airport, I don't think staff cared anymore about anything. The aviation companies were laying people off in the thousands. A job today might not be a job tomorrow. Nobody had the will or desire to raise an issue over luggage technicalities. The lady at the counter said nothing.

The lack of congestion in the terminal was a welcome sight, but not the closed lounges and duty-free stores, my usual refuges at any airport. In fact, no shop was open, and it was breakfast time. I was hungry and had to remain hungry. I did not eat until I was on the plane on the second leg of my journey, after the stopover in Frankfurt. And the airplane food had changed. There was no longer anything hot. All that was available were cold sandwiches and packaged snacks. There was also no booze, the only drink available being bottled water. The idea, I'm sure, was to minimize contact, whether it's between staff and passenger or between them and the food and drinks. This kind of inflight experience was fast becoming a worldwide trend, with everything pared down to the bare minimum and prices set to go up as airlines blocked the sale of seats next to each other so as to maintain physical distancing. Ireland's Ryanair, once infamous for considering standing-only flights and charging for the toilet, would even require customers to make a special request to use the washroom, like raising your hand in class. I couldn't help but think at least some of the less severe changes to air travel were here to stay. Travel is high-risk by nature, and that aspect is not going to change any time soon.

Compared to the shock I registered at being greeted by a sea of mask-wearing people upon arrival in Beijing, what I was now seeing on Air Canada on the trip home seemed all very normal to me—cabin staff in protective gear and wearing masks; formerly unimaginable or unacceptable rules being enforced and hardly given a second thought; and everyone moving super carefully around each other, like some mime exercise. This is what it is now, I thought. The new normal, to borrow an entirely over-used phrase. I didn't even mind the shoddy food that much. In fact, I've tasted nothing quite as good as that cold Air Canada turkey Caesar wrap.

———

According to my Google Maps tracking feature, I've spent so much time away from Toronto over the years that, aside from all the places I have lived in the city, my most frequently visited location is the airport. Arriving at Toronto's Pearson International Airport again and seeing it so starkly empty was jarring. I was tempted to cup my hands around my mouth and shout, "Ricola!"

Prior to coming to immigration, I was asked to fill out a form with my address and contact details, so that government workers could follow up to make sure I was self-isolating for fourteen days, as required for all incoming travellers. Once at the immigration counter, the officer made sure I understood the rules of self-isolation before letting me through. All said and done, it wasn't so bad—at least I didn't have a swab shoved through my nose like Risako, although the lack of any COVID-19 screening did surprise me a little.

With my landing back in Canada, I sort of felt like those astronauts who had spent more than two hundred days on the International Space Station only to return to Earth amid the worst days of the pandemic. They—two Americans and one Russian—had of course heard what was going on back on Earth, but seeing it in person was another thing entirely. It must all have seemed so strange and otherworldly. It certainly did for me. My experience of the pandemic's lockdown and disruption had happened only after I left home. Thus, in that base, instinctual part of my brain, it had been a foreign phenomenon. I did know on a rational level what was going on in Canada, what was closed, what was open, and the new dos and don'ts in society. But looking at it all from a distance had definitely been, in the words of one of the astronauts, "hard to understand." Seeing everything in person made it no easier.

After a week back in Toronto, a federal employee called to make sure I was, in fact, self-isolating for the required two-week period. She mispronounced my name in an oddly specific way, an error likely due to misreading my handwriting on the form I filled out upon arrival. An email later sent to me, with my named spelled exactly as she had pronounced it, confirmed my theory. That suggested the form was not cross-checked with electronic data or the border agency's records of who comes and goes. Maybe I could have written Michael Mouse and nobody would have been any the wiser. Anyway, I told the bureaucrat I was doing what I was told, which was the truth, and she was satisfied. She had been pulled off her normal duties to make these calls, she told me. During normal times, she had a different government job. I didn't ask what that was.

By then, the world already had more than 4 million infected and at least 300,000 dead. In Canada, it was some 70,000 infected and 5,000 dead. It got particularly bad in seniors' homes, whose residents are particularly vulnerable and where many live in confined environments. At one point, one-third of the virus deaths in the United States were linked to nursing homes. In Canada, nearly four in five deaths were associated with long-term care facilities. It got so bad, soldiers were called in to reinforce some of the homes, where it became clear how terribly underfunded and understaffed they were. A military report leaked to media detailed horrific conditions: residents left in soiled diapers or left crying for help for long periods, and around them, cock-roaches, flies, and rotten food. Medical supplies, including catheters, were allegedly reused, and "significant fecal contamination in numer-ous patient rooms" was found. Even in the higher-end ones, it was only a little better. In Montreal, an orderly at a long-term care centre wrote in her journal, published in a newspaper: "Ms. S, an 87-year-old patient, keeps saying how much she wants to die, how much she is tired of loneliness and confinement, how her loss of autonomy is driving her crazy and how she no longer feels a reason to live. She cries and asks for a hug." Ms. S died a few days later. In the orderly's journal, no cause was stated, but none was needed.

The news about the death toll and horrific conditions in long-term care facilities hit home for obvious reasons, but it turns out my grand-parents were okay. The seniors' residence they were in appears to have successfully locked down their environment, probably right after I walked out the front doors. The good news was that it had even started to allow visits again, although limited and only by appointment, and even-tually my grandmother had what she called a "very fortunate" day. She would finally get to see my Beijing uncle; my aunt, his elder sister; and my aunt's daughter again. "Lots of elderly still haven't seen their family, but they still hope for it every day," she would write in the family WeChat group. "They have to depend on the residence's staff for every-thing because 90 per cent of them do not have mobile phones."

My aunt posted a photo of my grandfather. He was little changed. Already ridden by both dementia and his failing body, he had been confined in the pandemic in a way that really wasn't any different from before. I wondered if he knew the chaos that had sprung around him, the lives lost and changed, the lockdown that had descended and left, and the upheaval that had come and would come again. I'm sure my grandmother talked to him, and that he could hear the newscasts she played and the small talk of the orderlies around and see that everyone was in face masks. My grandfather may not understand or retain much of anything, but I've come to believe there is a baser, more resilient part of his brain that took in the raw emotions of all of that, the sombreness of the television, the tension in the voices everywhere, and the cold emptiness of the room. I like to think he could feel the weight of the darkness, that he recognized it on some level, and that, in his own way, he resisted it. His toothless mouth agape in an almost hairless head, my grandfather had thus far weathered the pandemic largely unaffected, stubbornly and soundlessly, raging against the fates and the fading breath.

SELECTED BIBLIOGRAPHY

PROLOGUE AND PART ONE: YEAR OF THE RODENT

Agence France-Presse. "Beijing Reports Capital's First Death from Coronavirus." January 27, 2020.

British Broadcasting Corporation. "China Coronavirus: Death Toll Rises as Disease Spreads." January 25, 2020. https://www.bbc.com/news/world-asia-china-51245680.

Bowker, John, and Loni Prinsloo. "South African Airways Nears Collapse with Plan to Fire All Staff." *Bloomberg*, April 18, 2020. https://www.bloomberg.com/news/articles/2020-04-18/south-african-airways-nears-collapse-with-plan-to-fire-workforce.

Chambers, Madeline. "Germans Snitch on Neighbours Flouting Virus Rules, in Echo of the Stasi Past." *Reuters*, April 2, 2020. https://www.reuters.com/article/us-health-coronavirus-germany-denunciati/germans-snitch-on-neighbours-flouting-virus-rules-in-echo-of-the-stasi-past-idUSKBN21K2PB.

Chiang, Nora. "Middle-Class Taiwanese Immigrant Women Adapt to Life in Australasia: Case Studies from Transnational Households." *Asian Journal of Women's Studies* 10, no. 4 (January 2004): 31–57. https://doi.org/10.1080/12259276.2004.11665979.

Corkery, Michael, and David Yaffe-Bellany. "Meat Plant Closures Mean Pigs Are Gassed or Shot Instead." *New York Times*, May 14, 2020. https://www. nytimes.com/2020/05/14/business/coronavirus-farmers-killing-pigs.html.

Feng, Jiayun. "All the Hilariously Aggressive Coronavirus Propaganda Banners Found in China." *SupChina*, February 11, 2020. https://supchina.com/2020/ 02/11/all-the-hilariously-aggressive-coronavirus-banners-found-in-china.

Frost, Natasha. "All Over the World, Countries Are Imposing Travel Bans on Visitors Who've Been to China." *Quartz*, February 2, 2020. https://qz.com/ 1795615/coronavirus-travel-bans-on-china-imposed-by-growing-list-of-nations.

Fuller, Thomas, Mike Baker, Shawn Hubler, and Sheri Fink. "A Coronavirus Death in Early February Was 'Probably the Tip of an Iceberg.'" *New York Times*, April 22, 2020. https://www.nytimes.com/2020/04/22/us/santa-clara-county-coronavirus-death.html.

Goh, Timothy. "Man Who Breached Coronavirus Stay-Home Notice Stripped of Singapore PR Status, Barred from Re-Entry." *Straits Times*. https://www. straitstimes.com/singapore/coronavirus-singapore-permanent-resident-who-breached-stay-home-notice-stripped-of-pr.

Harari, Yuval Noah. "Yuval Noah Harari: The World after Coronavirus." *Financial Times*, March 20, 2020. https://www.ft.com/content/19d90308-6858-11ea-a3c9-1fe6fedcca75.

Hodge, James. "China's Mass Quarantines; Fifth Estate Investigation into Death of Preston Lochead; Hip Hop Ambassador Toni Blackman." *The Current*. Interviewed by Matt Galloway, January 24, 2020. https://www.cbc. ca/radio/thecurrent/the-current-for-jan-24-2020-1.5438975/friday-january-24-2020-full-transcript-1.5439431.

Kiernan, Samantha, and Madeleine DeVita. "Travel Restrictions on China due to COVID-19." *Think Global Health*, April 6, 2020. https://www. thinkglobalhealth.org/article/travel-restrictions-china-due-covid-19.

Kormann, Carolyn. "From Bats to Human Lungs, the Evolution of a Corona-virus." *New Yorker*, March 27, 2020. https://www.newyorker.com/science/elements/from-bats-to-human-lungs-the-evolution-of-a-coronavirus.

Lim, Min Zhang. "Coronavirus: SAF Helps with Contact Tracing, Calling Those on Stay-Home Notices." *Straits Times*, April 3, 2020. https://www.straitstimes.com/singapore/coronavirus-saf-helps-with-contact-tracing-calling-those-on-stay-home-notices.

Lou, Ethan. "Coronavirus in China: My Travels Through a Land in Lockdown." *Maclean's*, March 3, 2020. https://www.macleans.ca/politics/worldpolitics/coronavirus-in-china-my-travels-through-a-land-in-lockdown.

Malito, Alessandra. "'I Would Rather Him Be Lonely Than Dead': How to Manage When Someone You Love Is in a Nursing Home." *MarketWatch*, March 23, 2020. https://www.marketwatch.com/story/i-would-rather-him-be-lonely-than-dead-how-to-manage-when-someone-you-love-is-in-a-nursing-home-2020-03-18.

McDonnell, Tim. "What We've Learned from Past Pandemics." *Quartz*, March 17, 2020. https://qz.com/1820233/what-past-pandemics-can-teach-us-about-responding-to-coronavirus.

Merolla, Sabrina. "All China's Fast Food Dreams." *PRIVATE Photo Review*, January 14, 2015. https://www.privatephotoreview.com/2015/01/all-chinas-fast-food-dreams.

Moscow Times. "'Those Meant to Die Will Die,' Russia's Coronavirus Info Chief Says." May 20, 2020. https://www.themoscowtimes.com/2020/05/20/those-meant-to-die-will-die-russias-coronavirus-info-chief-says-a70322.

Onishi, Norimitsu, and Constant Méheut. "France Weighs Its Love of Liberty in Fight Against Coronavirus." *New York Times*, April 17, 2020. https://www.nytimes.com/2020/04/17/world/europe/coronavirus-france-digital-tracking.html.

Palma, Stefania. "How Singapore Waged War on Coronavirus." *Financial Times*, March 22, 2020. https://www.ft.com/content/ca4e0db0-6aaa-11ea-800d-da70cff6e4d3.

Patterson, Kevin. "Anatomy of a Pandemic." *The Walrus*, March 11, 2020. https://thewalrus.ca/anatomy-of-an-epidemic.

Qin, Amy, and Vivian Wang. "Wuhan, Center of Coronavirus Outbreak, Is Being Cut Off by Chinese Authorities." *New York Times*, January 22, 2020. https://www.nytimes.com/2020/01/22/world/asia/china-coronavirus-travel.html.

Salcedo, Andrea, Sanam Yar, and Gina Cherelus. "Coronavirus Travel Restrictions, Across the Globe." *New York Times*, May 8, 2020. https://www.nytimes.com/article/coronavirus-travel-restrictions.html.

Schaart, Eline. "Dutch Health Minister Collapses During Coronavirus Debate." *Politico*, March 18, 2020. https://www.politico.eu/article/dutch-health-minister-collapses-during-coronavirus-debate.

Schuetze, Christopher F. "Zoo May Feed Animals to Animals as Funds Dry Up in Pandemic." *New York Times*, April 15, 2020. https://www.nytimes.com/2020/04/15/world/europe/germany-zoo-coronavirus.html.

Secon, Holly, Aylin Woodward, and Dave Mosher. "A Comprehensive Timeline of the New Coronavirus Pandemic, from China's First Case to the Present." *Business Insider*, May 22, 2020. https://www.businessinsider.com/coronavirus-pandemic-timeline-history-major-events-2020-3.

Vaswani, Karishma. "Coronavirus: The Detectives Racing to Contain the Virus in Singapore." British Broadcasting Corporation, March 19, 2020. https://www.bbc.com/news/world-asia-51866102.

Zhong, Raymond, and Paul Mozur. "To Tame Coronavirus, Mao-Style Social Control Blankets China." *New York Times*, February 15, 2020. https://www.nytimes.com/2020/02/15/business/china-coronavirus-lockdown.html.

PART TWO: ANATOMY OF A CRISIS

Al-Arshani, Sarah. "US Coronavirus Models Increase Anticipated Death Toll to 74,000, the Second Increase in a Week as States Begin to Lift Stay-at-Home Orders." *Business Insider*, April 27, 2020. https://www.businessinsider.com/new-us-coronavirus-death-toll-models-estimate-deaths-august-2020-4.

Alchon, Suzanne Austin. *A Pest in the Land: New World Epidemics in a Global Perspective*. Albuquerque, New Mexico: University of New Mexico Press, 2003.

Allard, Tom, and Kate Lamb. "Exclusive: More Than 2,200 Indonesians Have Died with Coronavirus Symptoms, Data Shows." *Reuters*, April 27, 2020. https://www.reuters.com/article/us-health-coronavirus-indonesia-casualti/exclusive-more-than-2200-indonesians-have-died-with-coronavirus-symptoms-data-shows-idUSKCN22A04N.

Bailey, Mark. *The Decline of Serfdom in Late Medieval England: From Bondage to Freedom*. Woodbridge, United Kingdom: Boydell Press, 2014.

Belluz, Julia. "Why the Coronavirus Outbreak Might Be Much Bigger Than We Know." *Vox*, Feb. 14, 2020. https://www.vox.com/2020/2/14/21134473/coronavirus-outbreak-singapore-us-symptoms-pandemic.

Boccaccio, Giovanni. *The Decameron*. Translated by John Payne. New York, New York: Walter J. Black, 2007.

Boice, Jay. "Best-Case and Worst-Case Coronavirus Forecasts Are Very Far Apart." *FiveThirtyEight*, April 2, 2020. https://fivethirtyeight.com/features/best-case-and-worst-case-coronavirus-forecasts-are-very-far-apart.

Canadian Press. "Trudeau Speaks with First Ministers on Coronavirus, Promises Better Data Soon." *CityNews*, April 2, 2020. https://edmonton.citynews.ca/2020/04/02/trudeau-calls-first-ministers-meeting-on-coronavirus-promises-better-data-soon.

Clamp, Rachel. "Coronavirus and the Black Death: Spread of Misinformation and Xenophobia Shows We Haven't Learned from Our Past." *The*

Conversation, March 5, 2020. https://theconversation.com/coronavirus-and-the-black-death-spread-of-misinformation-and-xenophobia-shows-we-havent-learned-from-our-past-132802.

Cummins, Neil, Morgan Kelly, and Cormac Ó Gráda. "Coronavirus from the Perspective of 17th Century Plague." *Vox*, April 21, 2020. https://voxeu.org/article/coronavirus-perspective-17th-century-plague.

Daud, Sulaiman, and Kayla Wong. "Full Transcript of 25-minute Leaked Audio Recording of Chan Chun Sing Dialogue with SCCCI." *Mothership*, February 20, 2020. https://mothership.sg/2020/02/chan-chun-sing-leaked-transcript.

Duncan, Conrad. "Coronavirus: 70% of Population Likely to Be Infected, Experts Tell Angela Merkel." *The Independent*, March 11, 2020. https://www.independent.co.uk/news/world/europe/coronavirus-germany-news-angela-merkel-infected-population-experts-vaccine-a9394326.html.

Fink, Sheri. "Worst-Case Estimates for U.S. Coronavirus Deaths." *New York Times*, March 13, 2020. https://www.nytimes.com/2020/03/13/us/coronavirus-deaths-estimate.html.

Foucault, Michel. *Discipline and Punish: The Birth of the Prison*. Translated by Alan Sheridan. New York, New York: Vintage, 1995.

Getz, Faye Marie. "Black Death and the Silver Lining: Meaning, Continuity, and Revolutionary Change in Histories of Medieval Plague." *Journal of the History of Biology* 24 (June 1991): 265–89. https://doi.org/10.1007/BF00209432.

Giles, Chris. "UK Coronavirus Deaths More Than Double Official Figure, According to FT Study." *Financial Times*, April 21, 2020. https://www.ft.com/content/67e6a4ee-3d05-43bc-ba03-e239799fa6ab.

Haelle, Tara. "The COVID-19 Coronavirus Disease May Be Twice as Contagious as We Thought." *Forbes*, April 7, 2020. https://www.forbes.com/sites/tarahaelle/2020/04/07/the-covid19-coronavirus-disease-may-be-twice-as-contagious-as-we-thought/#242ea1a429a6.

Hajela, Deepti, Marina Villeneuve, and Karen Matthews. "Stark Disparities in New York City's Virus Toll." Associated Press, May 18, 2020. https://apnews.com/282c393552f8943206b67aeeaa0e1d2b.

Hammond, Mitchell. *Epidemics and the Modern World.* Toronto, Ontario: University of Toronto Press, 2019.

Henson, Bertha. "Virally speaking." *Bertha Harian* (blog), February 19, 2020. https://berthahenson.wordpress.com/2020/02/19/virally-speaking.

Hohman, Maura. "Airline Says Passengers Must Ask to Use the Bathroom on Upcoming Flights." *Today,* May 19, 2020. https://www.today.com/news/ryanair-has-new-bathroom-protocol-flights-during-coronavirus-t181926.

James, Tom. "Black Death: The Lasting Impact." British Broadcasting Corporation, February 17, 2020. http://www.bbc.co.uk/history/british/middle_ages/black_impact_01.shtml.

Katz, Josh, and Margot Sanger-Katz. "Deaths in New York City Are More Than Double the Usual Total." *New York Times,* April 10, 2020. https://www.nytimes.com/interactive/2020/04/10/upshot/coronavirus-deaths-new-york-city.html.

Knight, Sam. "Reading About the Black Death with My Daughter During the Coronavirus Outbreak." *New Yorker,* March 14, 2020. https://www.newyorker.com/news/letter-from-the-uk/reading-about-the-black-death-with-my-daughter-during-the-coronavirus-outbreak.

LeBlanc, Paul. "US Coronavirus Predictions Are Shifting. Here's Why." CNN, April 9, 2020. https://edition.cnn.com/2020/04/08/politics/what-matters-april-8.

Little, Simon. "Approval of Prime Minister, Premiers Soars Amid Coronavirus Response: Ipsos Poll." *Global News,* April 8, 2020. https://globalnews.ca/news/6792350/coronavirus-poll-prime-minster-premier-approvals/.619wellington.

Mark, Joshua J. "Effects of the Black Death on Europe." Ancient History

Encyclopedia, April 16, 2020. https://www.ancient.eu/article/1543/effects-of-the-black-death-on-europe.

McKinley, Kathryn. "How the Rich Reacted to the Bubonic Plague has Eerie Similarities to Today's Pandemic." *The Conversation*, April 16, 2020. https://theconversation.com/how-the-rich-reacted-to-the-bubonic-plague-has-eerie-similarities-to-todays-pandemic-135925.

Merelli, Annalisa. "Hysteria Over Coronavirus in Italy Is Reminiscent of the Black Death." *Quartz*, February 24, 2020. https://qz.com/1807049/hysteria-over-coronavirus-in-italy-is-reminiscent-of-the-black-death.

Mintz, Luke. "From Shakespeare to Newton, Britain's Great Thinkers Did Some of Their Best Work Under Lockdown." *The Telegraph*, April 20, 2020. https://www.telegraph.co.uk/health-fitness/body/shakespeare-newton-britains-great-thinkers-did-best-work-lockdown.

National Post. "Coronavirus Live Updates: Life Won't Return to Normal Until We Have a Vaccine—12 to 18 Months, Trudeau Says." April 9, 2020. https://nationalpost.com/news/canada/coronavirus-live-updates-covid-19-covid19.

Olaya, Vicente G. "The Surprising Similarities Between the Coronavirus and the Bubonic Plague." *El Pais*, April 21, 2020. https://english.elpais.com/society/2020-04-21/the-surprising-similarities-between-the-coronavirus-and-the-bubonic-plague.html.

Pan, Jie. "An Attempt to Understand Why So Many People Dislike Minister Chan Chun Sing." *Rice*, December 15, 2018. https://www.ricemedia.co/current-affairs-commentary-understanding-dislike-minister-chan-chun-sing.

Pappas, Stephanie. "Black Death Likely Altered European Genes." *Live Science*, February 3, 2014. https://www.livescience.com/43063-black-death-roma-evolution.html.

———, "It Got Better: Life Improved After Black Death, Study Finds." *Live Science*, May 7, 2014. https://www.livescience.com/45428-health-improved-black-death.html.

Pluess, Jessica Davis. "The Mystical and Mythical Edelweiss." *House of Switzerland*, July 8, 2018. https://www.houseofswitzerland.org/swissstories/history/mystical-and-mythical-edelweiss.

Purnell, Newley. "Singapore Has the Most Expensive Beer in Asia." *Quartz*, December 6, 2013. https://qz.com/155057/singapore-has-the-most-expensive-beer-in-asia.

Quealy, Kevin. "The Richest Neighborhoods Emptied Out Most as Coronavirus Hit New York City." *New York Times*, May 15, 2020. https://www.nytimes.com/interactive/2020/05/15/upshot/who-left-new-york-coronavirus.html.

Sales-Carbonell, Jordina. "La 'plaga de Justinià' segons el testimoni de Procopi." *Epidèmies a l'Edat Mitjana* (blog), April 3, 2020. https://epidemiesedatmitjana.wordpress.com/2020/04/03/la-plaga-de-justinia-segons-el-testimoni-de-procopi.

Saul, Toby. "Inside the Swift, Deadly History of the Spanish Flu Pandemic." *National Geographic*, March 4, 2018. https://www.nationalgeographic.com/history/magazine/2018/03-04/history-spanish-flu-pandemic.

Schnoor, Aaron. "Is the Coronavirus the New Black Plague?" *Medium*, March 5, 2020. https://medium.com/lessons-from-history/is-the-coronavirus-the-new-black-plague-31f93d2bbfd6.

Shipman, Pat Lee. "The Bright Side of the Black Death." *American Scientist* 102, no. 6 (November 2014): 410. https://doi.org/10.1511/2014.111.410.

Snowden, Frank. *Epidemics and Society: From the Black Death to the Present*. New Haven, Connecticut: Yale University Press, 2020.

Sridhar, Devi. "Britain Must Change Course — And Resume Covid-19 Testing to Protect Frontline NHS Staff." *The Guardian*, March 16, 2020. https://www.theguardian.com/commentisfree/2020/mar/16/resume-covid-19-testing-protect-frontline-nhs-staff.

Stamataki, Zania. "Why Is Coronavirus So Frighteningly Successful?" *The Guardian*, April 20, 2020. https://www.theguardian.com/commentisfree/2020/apr/20/coronavirus-master-of-disguise-scientists-viruses-covid-19.

Tan, Martino. "Leaked Audio of Singlish-Spewing Chan Chun Sing Impresses & Dismays S'poreans at the Same Time." *Mothership*, February 20, 2020. https://mothership.sg/2020/02/chan-chun-sing-leaked.

Walsh, Bryan. "The Medieval Black Death Made You Healthier—If You Survived." *Time*, May 7, 2014. https://time.com/91315/the-medieval-black-death-made-you-healthier-if-you-survived.

Wisecrack. "How Pandemics Change Society—Wisecrack Edition." YouTube video, April 13, 2020. https://www.youtube.com/watch?v=2Rr9b-HMSS4.

York, Geoffrey. "The COVID-19 Pandemic Could Be 'Devastating' for Battles against Tuberculosis, HIV and Malaria." *Globe and Mail*, May 22, 2020. https://www.theglobeandmail.com/world/article-the-covid-19-pandemic-could-be-devastating-for-battles-against.

Young, Chris. "Comparing the Wuhan Coronavirus to 6 Other Deadly Outbreaks." *Interesting Engineering*, February 11, 2020. https://interestingengineering.com/comparing-the-wuhan-coronavirus-to-6-other-deadly-outbreaks.

PART THREE: RIPPLES ACROSS THE POND

Acocella, Joan. "The End of the World: Interpreting the Plague" *New Yorker*, March 14, 2005. https://www.newyorker.com/magazine/2005/03/21/the-end-of-the-world.

Al Jazeera. "WHO Warns Europe Is Coronavirus 'Epicentre' as Cases, Deaths Rise." March 13, 2020. https://www.aljazeera.com/news/2020/03/warns-europe-epicentre-pandemic-cases-deaths-rise-200313170721317.html.

Baran, Michelle. "The U.S. Ban on Travel Now Includes Europe, the U.K., and Ireland—What You Need to Know." *AFAR*, March 14, 2020. https://www.afar.com/magazine/the-us-ban-on-travel-from-europe-what-you-need-to-know.

Bavarian Ministerial Gazette. "Emergency Notice." April 16, 2020. https://home.army.mil/bavaria/application/files/6815/8713/3819/coronavirus_Bavaria_ordinance_16Apr2020.pdf.

Blyth, Mark, and Eric Lonergan. "This Time, Can We Finally Turn a Financial Crisis into an Opportunity?" *Foreign Policy*, March 20, 2020. https://foreignpolicy.com/2020/03/20/this-time-can-we-finally-turn-a-financial-crisis-into-an-opportunity.

Canadian Broadcasting Corporation. "John Tory Says City Forced to Contemplate 'Devastating' Service Cuts Without Federal, Provincial Funding." May 22, 2020. https://www.cbc.ca/news/canada/toronto/toronto-covid-19-may-22-1.5580045.

Carney, Jordain. "Harris, Sanders, Markey Propose $2,000 Monthly Payments Amid Coronavirus Pandemic." *The Hill*, May 8, 2020. https://thehill.com/homenews/senate/496747-harris-sanders-markey-propose-2000-monthly-payments-amid-coronavirus-pandemic.

Chor, Laurel (@laurelchor). "At the airport, staff made sure I scanned a QR code and downloaded the app, which was then registered to my phone # and my tracking bracelet. I had to let the app know when I got home from the airport." Twitter post, May 14, 2020. https://twitter.com/laurelchor/status/1260911916488093697.

Clark, Campbell. "It's the Provinces That Will Emerge from This Crisis Weaker, as Power Shifts to Ottawa." *Globe and Mail*, May 22, 2020. https://www.theglobeandmail.com/politics/article-its-the-provinces-that-will-emerge-from-this-crisis-weaker-as-power.

Clifford, Catherine. "Pope Francis: 'This May Be the Time to Consider a Universal Basic Wage.'" CNBC, April 13, 2020. https://www.cnbc.com/2020/04/13/pope-francis-it-may-be-the-time-to-consider-a-universal-basic-wage.html.

Cowles, Charlotte. "With Interest: Failing to Save Jobs." *New York Times*, June 28, 2020.

Cullen, Paul. "Ireland Is 'Exactly 14 Days Behind Italy' in Terms of Coronavirus Cases." *Irish Times*, March 13, 2020. https://www.irishtimes.com/news/health/

ireland-is-exactly-14-days-behind-italy-in-terms-of-coronavirus-cases-1.4202013.

Donadio, Rachel. "Italy's Coronavirus Response Is a Warning from the Future." *The Atlantic*, March 8, 2020. https://www.theatlantic.com/international/ archive/2020/03/italy-coronavirus-covid19-west-europe-future/607660.

Duhigg, Charles, and Keith Bradsher. "How the U.S. Lost Out on iPhone Work." *New York Times*, January 21, 2012. https://www.nytimes.com/2012/01/ 22/business/apple-america-and-a-squeezed-middle-class.html.

Dyer, Evan. "From Pipe Dream to Prospect: The Pandemic Is Making a Case for a Universal Basic Income." Canadian Broadcasting Corporation, April 19, 2020. https://www.cbc.ca/news/politics/universal-basic-income-covid-coronavirus-pandemic-1.5536144.

Eisenberg, Merle, Lee Mordechai, and Robert Alpert. "Why Treating the Coronavirus Like the Black Death Is So Dangerous." *Washington Post*, February 6, 2020. https://www.washingtonpost.com/outlook/2020/02/06/why-treating-coronavirus-like-black-death-is-so-dangerous.

Eisinger, Jesse. "How the Coronavirus Bailout Repeats 2008's Mistakes: Huge Corporate Payoffs with Little Accountability." *ProPublica*, April 7, 2020. https://www.propublica.org/article/how-the-coronavirus-bailout-repeats-2008s-mistakes-huge-corporate-payoffs-with-little-accountability.

Ellis-Petersen, Hannah. "Rodrigo Duterte's Drug War Is 'Large-Scale Murdering Enterprise' Says Amnesty." *The Guardian*, July 8, 2019. https://www. theguardian.com/world/2019/jul/08/rodrigo-dutertes-drug-war-is-large-scale-murdering-enterprise-says-amnesty.

Erdbrink, Thomas, and Christina Anderson. "'Life Has to Go On': How Sweden Has Faced the Virus Without a Lockdown." *New York Times*, April 28, 2020. https://www.nytimes.com/by/thomas-erdbrink.

Erskine-Smith, Nathaniel. "Is It Time for a Basic Income? with Evelyn Forget" *Uncommons: Canadian Politics With Nathaniel Erskine-Smith*, March 26, 2020. Podcast. https://podcastaddict.com/podcast/2728853.

Fawcett, Max. "How Universal Basic Income Will Save the Economy." *The Walrus*, May 4, 2020. https://thewalrus.ca/how-universal-basic-income-will-save-the-economy.

Garcia, Mario R. "Does Creativity Suffer When Design Is Outsourced?" *The Mario Blog*, February 19, 2018. https://www.garciamedia.com/blog/does-creativity-suffer-when-design-is-outsourced.

Gebrekidan, Selam. "For Autocrats, and Others, Coronavirus Is a Chance to Grab Even More Power." *New York Times*, March 30, 2020. https://www.nytimes.com/2020/03/30/world/europe/coronavirus-governments-power.html.

Guardian (Prince Edward Island). "EDITORIAL: Too Good to Give Up." Saltwire Network, April 29, 2020. https://www.saltwire.com/opinion/local-perspectives/editorial-too-good-to-give-up-443520.

Guest, Dennis. "Family Allowance." *Canadian Encyclopedia*, February 7, 2006. https://thecanadianencyclopedia.ca/en/article/family-allowance.

Howlett, Karen, Laura Stone, Jill Mahoney, and Tu Thanh Ha. "Ontario to Take Control of Five Long-Term Care Homes After Military Report Citing Neglect, Abuse." *Globe and Mail*, May 27, 2020. https://www.theglobeandmail.com/canada/article-ontario-to-take-control-of-five-long-term-care-homes-after-military.

Ibbitson, John. "This Pandemic Will Reshape the Social Landscape — It's Just Too Soon to Say How." *Globe and Mail*, March 29, 2020. https://www.theglobeandmail.com/opinion/article-this-pandemic-will-reshape-the-social-landscape-its-just-too-soon.

Kirkpatrick, Tim. "This Is the Flower That Marked a German Soldier as Being Elite." *We Are the Mighty*, June 29, 2018. https://www.wearethemighty.com/history/edelweiss-flower-german-elite-troops#:~:text=The%20edelweiss%2C%20otherwise%20known%20as,'noble'%20and%20'white.

Kosnar, Michael, and Pete Williams. "Pandemic Pushes U.S. Gun Sales to

All-Time High." NBC, April 3, 2020. https://www.nbcnews.com/politics/
politics-news/pandemic-pushes-u-s-gun-sales-all-time-high-n1176451.

Lee, Yen Nee. "5 Charts Show Why the Global Economy Is More Vulnerable
Now Than During SARS." CNBC, February 4, 2020. https://www.cnbc.com/
2020/02/05/coronavirus-how-china-economy-has-changed-since-sars.html.

MacMillan, Margaret. "Making History: How a Pandemic Took the World
by Surprise." *Globe and Mail*, May 8, 2020. https://www.theglobeandmail.
com/opinion/article-making-history-how-a-pandemic-took-the-world-by-
surprise.

Maheshwari, Sapna, and Michael Corkery. "U.S. Retail Crisis Deepens as
Hundreds of Thousands Lose Work." *New York Times*. March 30, 2020.
https://www.nytimes.com/2020/03/30/business/coronavirus-retail-fur-
loughs-macys.html.

Maheshwari, Sapna, and Vanessa Friedman. "The Death of the Department
Store: 'Very Few Are Likely to Survive.'" *New York Times*, April 21, 2020.
https://www.nytimes.com/2020/04/21/business/coronavirus-department-
stores-neiman-marcus.html.

Markowitz, Shane. "Why Trump Has Received a Much Smaller Approval
Bump Than Other World Leaders During the Pandemic." *Washington
Post*, April 8, 2020. https://www.washingtonpost.com/politics/2020/04/08/
why-trumps-received-much-smaller-approval-bump-than-other-world-
leaders-during-pandemic.

Mason, Gary. "The Next COVID-19 Crisis? Canada's Cash-Strapped Cities."
Globe and Mail, April 14, 2020. https://www.theglobeandmail.com/opinion/
article-the-next-covid-19-crisis-canadas-cash-strapped-cities.

Matthews, Dylan. "Mitt Romney's Coronavirus Economic Plan: $1,000 to
Each American Adult." *Vox*, March 16, 2020. https://www.vox.com/future-
perfect/2020/3/16/21181872/mitt-romney-ubi-coronavirus-economic-plan-
andrew-yang.

Maxouris, Christina, and Joe Sutton. "These Astronauts Just Returned to Earth to Find a World Now Transformed by the Coronavirus." CNN, April 17, 2020. https://www.cnn.com/2020/04/17/world/astronauts-return-earth-coronavirus-scn/index.html.

McPhillips, Deidre. "Survey: Majority of Americans Don't Trust Government with Their Health." *U.S. News*, March 26, 2020. https://www.usnews.com/news/best-countries/articles/2020-03-26/survey-shows-potential-link-between-trust-in-government-coronavirus-response.

Orihuela, Rodrigo. "Spanish Government Aims to Roll Out Basic Income 'Soon.'" *Bloomberg*, April 5, 2020. https://www.bloomberg.com/news/articles/2020-04-05/spanish-government-aims-to-roll-out-basic-income-soon.

Patel, Raisa. "Canadian Travellers Should Return Home While They Still Can, Champagne Recommends." Canadian Broadcasting Corporation, March 14, 2020. https://www.cbc.ca/news/politics/canadian-travellers-abroad-should-return-home-champagne-says-1.5498252.

Paumgarten, Nick. "The Price of the Coronavirus Pandemic." *New Yorker*. April 13, 2020. https://www.newyorker.com/magazine/2020/04/20/the-price-of-the-coronavirus-pandemic.

"Public Health in Wartime. January 1940." *Canadian Public Health Journal* 31, no. 1 (1940): 35–36. www.jstor.org/stable/41978002.

Purdue, A. W. "The Transformative Impact of World War II." European History Online, April 18, 2016. http://ieg-ego.eu/en/threads/alliances-and-wars/war-as-an-agent-of-transfer/a-w-purdue-the-transformative-impact-of-world-war-ii.

Read, Leonard E. "I, Pencil: My Family Tree as Told to Leonard E. Read." *The Freeman* (December 1958).

Sherwood, Dave. "Chile to Push Ahead with Coronavirus 'Release Certificates' Despite WHO Warning." *Reuters*, April 26, 2020. https://www.reuters.com/

article/us-health-coronavirus-chile/chile-to-push-ahead-with-coronavirus-release-certificates-despite-who-warning-idUSKCN2280NW.

Snowden, Frank. "Coronavirus Is Not Just a Tragedy. It's an Opportunity to Build a Better World." Interview by Roge Karma. *Vox*, April 10, 2020. https://www.vox.com/2020/4/10/21213287/coronavirus-covid-19-pandemic-epidemic-society-historian-nationalism-globalization.

Specia, Megan. "Duterte, Philippine President, Boasts He Killed Someone as a Teenager." *New York Times*, November 10, 2017. https://www.nytimes.com/2017/11/10/world/asia/philippines-president-duterte-killed.html.

Spector, Mike. "Luxury Retailer Neiman Marcus Files for Bankruptcy Amid COVID-19 Pandemic." *Reuters*, May 7, 2020. https://www.reuters.com/article/us-neimanmarcus-bankruptcy/luxury-retailer-neiman-marcus-files-for-bankruptcy-amid-covid-19-pandemic-idUSKBN22J2AJ.

Stone, Jon. "Spain Gets New Left-Wing Coalition Government After Socialist Leader Wins Vote." *The Independent*, January 7, 2020. https://www.independent.co.uk/news/world/europe/spain-parliament-election-pedro-sanchez-left-wing-coalition-latest-a9273756.html.

Thwaites, Thomas. *The Toaster Project: Or a Heroic Attempt to Build a Simple Electric Appliance from Scratch*. Hudson, New York: Princeton Architectural Press, 2011.

Tooze, Adam. "The Normal Economy Is Never Coming Back." *Foreign Policy*, April 9, 2020. https://foreignpolicy.com/2020/04/09/unemployment-coronavirus-pandemic-normal-economy-is-never-coming-back.

———, "Shockwave." *London Review of Books* 42, no. 8 (April 16, 2020). https://www.lrb.co.uk/the-paper/v42/n08/adam-tooze/shockwave?referrer=https%3A%2F%2Fwww.google.com%2F.

Valpy, Michael, and Frank Graves. "Canadians Are Telling Their Government —Do Whatever It Takes to Make It Right." *Maclean's*, March 31, 2020.

https://www.macleans.ca/opinion/canadians-are-telling-their-government-do-whatever-it-takes-to-make-it-right.

York, Geoffrey. "Africa's Biggest Economy Faces a Double Blow from Oil Crisis and Surging Pandemic." *Globe and Mail*, May 14, 2020. https://www.theglobeandmail.com/business/article-africas-biggest-economy-faces-a-double-blow-from-oil-crisis-and.

PART FOUR: DEATH OF A (GLOBAL) VILLAGE

Adler, Katya. "Coronavirus: Can EU Get a Grip on Crisis?" British Broadcasting Corporation, March 27, 2020. https://www.bbc.com/news/world-europe-52058742.

Al Jazeera. "World Reacts to Trump Withdrawing WHO Funding." April 15, 2020. https://www.aljazeera.com/news/2020/04/world-reacts-trump-withdrawing-funding-200415061612025.html.

Anderson, Bruce. "The New World Order Is Disorder." *National Observer*, May 25, 2020. https://www.nationalobserver.com/2020/05/25/opinion/new-world-order-disorder.

Anti-Defamation League (blog). "Coronavirus: Antisemitism." April 22, 2020. https://www.adl.org/blog/coronavirus-antisemitism.

———, "Coronavirus: Anti-Immigration, Xenophobia and Homophobia." April 21, 2020. https://www.adl.org/blog/coronavirus-anti-immigration-xenophobia-and-homophobia.

Apuzzo, Matt. "Pressured by China, E.U. Softens Report on Covid-19 Disinformation." *New York Times*, April 24, 2020. https://www.nytimes.com/2020/04/24/world/europe/disinformation-china-eu-coronavirus.html.

Aurelius, Marcus. *Meditations*. Translated by George Long. Harvard University. Accessed May 10, 2020.

Brandt, Jessica, Bret Schafer. "Five Things to Know About Beijing's Disinformation Approach." *Alliance for Securing Democracy*, March 30, 2020.

https://securingdemocracy.gmfus.org/five-things-to-know-about-beijings-disinformation-approach.

Buttigieg, Pete. "Pete Buttigieg: China Wants Four More Years of Trump." *Washington Post*, May 1, 2020. https://www.washingtonpost.com/outlook/2020/05/01/trump-china-biden-election.

Cavallaro, Federico, and Alberto Dianin. "Cross-Border Commuting in Central Europe: Features, Trends and Policies." *Transport Policy* 78 (June 2019): 86–104. https://doi.org/10.1016/j.tranpol.2019.04.008.

Communications Security Establishment and Canadian Security Intelligence Service. "Joint CSE and CSIS Statement." May 14, 2020. https://www.cse-cst.gc.ca/en/media/2020-05-14.

de la Bruyere, Emily, and Nathan Picarsic. "Viral Moment: China's Post-COVID Planning." Horizon Advisory, March 15, 2020. https://www.horizonadvisory.org/news/coronavirus-series-report-launch-viral-moment-chinas-post-covid-planning.

Deutsche Welle. "Coronavirus: German President Urges European Solidarity." March 26, 2020. https://www.dw.com/en/coronavirus-german-president-urges-european-solidarity/a-52923741.

———, "Germany Enters Recession Due to Coronavirus." May 25, 2020. https://www.dw.com/en/germany-enters-recession-due-to-coronavirus/a-53556594.

Duclos, Michel. "Is COVID-19 a Geopolitical Game-Changer?" *Institut Montaigne*, March 24, 2020. https://www.institutmontaigne.org/en/blog/covid-19-geopolitical-game-changer.

Emmott, Robin. "Russia Deploying Coronavirus Disinformation to Sow Panic in West, EU Document Says." *Reuters*, March 18, 2020. https://www.reuters.com/article/us-health-coronavirus-disinformation/russia-deploying-corona-virus-disinformation-to-sow-panic-in-west-eu-document-says-idUSK-BN21518F.

European Commission. "Travel to and from the EU During the Pandemic." Accessed June 11, 2020. https://ec.europa.eu/info/live-work-travel-eu/health/coronavirus-response/travel-and-transportation-during-coronavirus-pandemic/travel-and-eu-during-pandemic_en#travel-restrictions.

Farrell, Henry, and Abraham Newman. "Will the Coronavirus End Globalization as We Know It?" *Foreign Affairs*, March 16, 2020. https://www.foreignaffairs.com/articles/2020-03-16/will-coronavirus-end-globalization-we-know-it.

Faulconbridge, Guy. "George Soros says EU May Not Survive Coronavirus Crisis." *Reuters*, May 22, 2020. https://www.reuters.com/article/us-health-coronavirus-eu-soros/george-soros-says-eu-may-not-survive-coronavirus-crisis-idUSKBN22Y168.

Fife, Robert, and Michelle Zilio. "Freeland Questions U.S. Leadership, Says Canada Must Set Own Course." *Globe and Mail*, June 6, 2017. https://www.theglobeandmail.com/news/politics/canada-must-re-invest-in-military-as-us-withdraws-from-world-freeland-says/article35212024.

Froelich, Paula. "Bolivian Orchestra Stranded at 'Haunted' German Castle Surrounded by Wolves." *New York Post*, May 23, 2020." https://nypost.com/2020/05/23/bolivian-orchestra-stuck-at-german-castle-surrounded-by-wolves.

Galston, William A. "Efficiency Isn't the Only Economic Virtue." *Wall Street Journal*, March 10, 2020. https://www.wsj.com/articles/efficiency-isnt-the-only-economic-virtue-11583873155.

Gerrand, Vivian. "Resilience, Radicalisation and Democracy in the COVID-19 Pandemic." *openDemocracy*, April 2, 2020. https://www.opendemocracy.net/en/global-extremes/resilience-radicalisation-and-democracy-covid-19-pandemic.

Giglio, Mike. "China's Spies Are on the Offensive." *The Atlantic*, August 26, 2019. https://www.theatlantic.com/politics/archive/2019/08/inside-us-china-espionage-war/595747.

Gingerich, Jon. "Students Can't Tell Difference Between Fake, Real News."

O'Dwyer's, December 5, 2019. https://www.odwyerpr.com/story/public/13486/ 2019-12-05/students-cant-tell-difference-between-fake-real-news.html.

Glavin, Terry. "The Coronavirus Pandemic Is the Breakthrough Xi Jinping Has Been Waiting For." Maclean's, April 3, 2020. https://www.macleans.ca/ opinion/the-coronavirus-pandemic-is-the-breakthrough-xi-jinping-has-been-waiting-for-and-hes-making-his-move.

Hernández-Morales, Aitor. "Germany Confirms That Trump Tried to Buy Firm Working on Coronavirus Vaccine." Politico, March 15, 2020. https:// www.politico.eu/article/germany-confirms-that-donald-trump-tried-to-buy-firm-working-on-coronavirus-vaccine.

Human Rights Watch. "Covid-19 Fueling Anti-Asian Racism and Xenophobia Worldwide." May 12, 2020. https://www.hrw.org/news/2020/05/12/covid-19-fueling-anti-asian-racism-and-xenophobia-worldwide.

Kao, Jeff, and Mia Shuang Li. "How China Built a Twitter Propaganda Machine Then Let It Loose on Coronavirus." ProPublica, March 26, 2020. https://www.propublica.org/article/how-china-built-a-twitter-propaganda-machine-then-let-it-loose-on-coronavirus.

Kauffmann, Sylvie. "Can Europe Stay Back from the Brink?" New York Times, May 22, 2020. https://www.nytimes.com/2020/05/22/opinion/europe-back-from-brink.html.

Kim, Catherine. "Hong Kong Declares a State of Emergency in Response to Five Confirmed Coronavirus Cases." Vox, January 25, 2020. https://www. vox.com/2020/1/25/21081400/coronavirus-cases-hong-kong-emergency.

Kissinger, Henry A. "The Coronavirus Pandemic Will Forever Alter the World Order." Wall Street Journal, April 3, 2020. https://www.wsj.com/articles/the-coronavirus-pandemic-will-forever-alter-the-world-order-11585953005.

Kolga, Marcus, Kaveh Shahrooz, and Shuvaloy Majumdar. "How China Weaponized Its Supply Chain." Maclean's, April 7, 2020. https://www.macleans. ca/opinion/how-china-weaponized-its-supply-chain.

Kuo, Lily. "'American Coronavirus': China Pushes Propaganda Casting Doubt on Virus Origin." *The Guardian*, March 13, 2020. https://www.theguardian.com/world/2020/mar/12/conspiracy-theory-that-coronavirus-originated-in-us-gaining-traction-in-china.

Kuper, Simon. "The Pandemic Will Forever Transform How We Live." *Financial Times*, April 8, 2020. https://www.ft.com/content/06647198-77b9-11ea-9840-1b8019d9a987.

Lytvynenko, Jane. "Chinese State Media Spread a False Image of a Hospital for Coronavirus Patients in Wuhan." *BuzzFeed News*, January 27, 2020. https://www.buzzfeednews.com/article/janelytvynenko/china-state-media-false-coronavirus-hospital-image.

Massari, Maurizio. "Italian Ambassador to the EU: Italy Needs Europe's Help." *Politico*, March 10, 2020. https://www.politico.eu/article/coronavirus-italy-needs-europe-help.

Merkel, Angela. "This Is a Historic Task—And It Can Only Be Mastered If We Face It Together" (Speech). March 18, 2020. Federal Chancellery, Berlin, Germany. Video with transcript, 12:43, https://www.americanrhetoric.com/speeches/angelamerkelcoronavirusaddresstonation.htm.

Morris, Loveday, Luisa Beck, and Rick Noack. "Merkel Says Coronavirus Presents Gravest Crisis Since WWII." *Washington Post*, March 18, 2020. https://www.washingtonpost.com/world/europe/germany-coronavirus-merkel/2020/03/18/9f34f2aa-6880-11ea-b199-3a9799c54512_story.html.

Moss, Gail. "Cross-Border Commuting: So Near and Yet So Far." *IPE*, January 2016. https://www.ipe.com/cross-border-commuting-so-near-and-yet-so-far/10011303.article.

Perper, Rosie. "China Is Injecting Millions into WHO as the US Cuts Funds. Experts Say Beijing Is Trying to Boost Its Influence Over the Agency and Its 'Deeply Compromised' Chief." *Business Insider*, April 24, 2020. https://

www.businessinsider.com/china-who-multimillion-dollar-contribution-political-power-move-2020-4.

Rana, Preetika, and Denise Roland. "Drugmakers Gain More Access to China, but at a Price." *Wall Street Journal*, November 27, 2018. https://www.wsj.com/articles/china-opens-door-to-foreign-drugs-for-a-discount-1543320003.

Rinke, Andreas, and Paul Carrel. "Germany Tries to Stop US from Luring Away Firm Seeking Coronavirus Vaccine." *Reuters*, March 15, 2020. https://www.reuters.com/article/health-coronavirus-germany-usa/germany-tries-to-stop-us-from-luring-away-firm-seeking-coronavirus-vaccine-idUSL8N2B8075.

Roland, Denise, and Jared S. Hopkins. "FDA Cites Shortage of One Drug, Exposing Supply-Line Worry." *Wall Street Journal*, February 28, 2020. https://www.wsj.com/articles/coronavirus-slows-drug-production-in-china-the-worlds-pharmacy-11582900885.

Satter, Raphael, Robin Emmott, and Jack Stubbs. "China Pressured EU to Drop COVID Disinformation Criticism: Sources." *Reuters*, April 24. 2020. https://www.reuters.com/article/us-health-coronavirus-eu-china/china-pressured-eu-to-drop-covid-disinformation-criticism-sources-idUSKCN227030.

Spengler, Oswald. *The Decline of the West*. Translated by Charles Francis Atkinson. New York, New York: Vintage, 2016.

Sukhankin, Sergey. "COVID-19 as a Tool of Information Confrontation: Russia's Approach." School of Public Policy, University of Calgary, April 2020. https://www.policyschool.ca/events/covid-19-as-a-tool-of-information-confrontation-russias-approach.

Sutton, Candace. "Australia Was Drained of Masks for China." *Chronicle*, March 26, 2020. https://www.thechronicle.com.au/news/australia-was-drained-of-masks-for-china/3981857.

Stein, Jeff. "FBI's Russia Probe Expands to Include 'Pizza Gate' Threats." *Newsweek*, March 22, 2017. https://www.newsweek.com/pizzagate-trump-russia-clinton-podesta-comet-ping-pong-pedophiles-david-seaman-572578.

Stevis-Gridneff, Matina, and Lara Jakes. "World Leaders Join to Pledge $8 Billion for Vaccine as U.S. Goes It Alone." *New York Times*, May 4, 2020. https://www.nytimes.com/2020/05/04/world/europe/eu-coronavirus-vaccine.html.

Swanson, Ana. "Coronavirus Spurs U.S. Efforts to End China's Chokehold on Drugs." *New York Times*, March 11, 2020. https://www.nytimes.com/2020/03/11/business/economy/coronavirus-china-trump-drugs.html.

The Telegraph. "Lee Kuan Yew, Asian Statesman—Obituary." March 23, 2015. https://www.telegraph.co.uk/news/obituaries/11437131/Lee-Kuan-Yew-Asian-statesman-obituary.html.

Thiessen, Marc A. "China Is Using Covid-19 to Throttle Hong Kong's Pro-Democracy Movement." *Washington Post*, May 21, 2020. https://www.washingtonpost.com/opinions/2020/05/21/china-is-using-covid-19-throttle-hong-kongs-pro-democracy-movement.

Tsang, Amie. "E.U. Seeks Solidarity as Nations Restrict Medical Exports." *New York Times*, March 7, 2020. https://www.nytimes.com/2020/03/07/business/eu-exports-medical-equipment.html.

Vogel, Peter. "Nationalism: The Even Greater Risk of the COVID-19 Crisis?" *IMD*, March 2020. https://www.imd.org/research-knowledge/articles/Nationalism-the-even-greater-risk-of-the-COVID-19-crisis.

Walker, Shaun. "The Humiliation That Pushed Putin to Try and Recapture Russian Glory." *History*, February 23, 2018. https://www.history.com/news/vladimir-putin-russia-power.

Wardle, Claire. "Misinformation Has Created a New World Disorder." *Scientific American*, September 1, 2019. https://www.scientificamerican.com/article/misinformation-has-created-a-new-world-disorder.

Wells, Paul. "Can the Forces of Globalization Ever Hope to Outlast the Corona-virus?" *Maclean's*, April 6, 2020. https://www.macleans.ca/politics/worldpolitics/can-the-forces-of-globalization-ever-hope-to-beat-the-coronavirus.

Westcott, Ben, and Steven Jiang. "Chinese Diplomat Promotes Conspiracy Theory That US Military Brought Coronavirus to Wuhan." CNN, March 13, 2020. https://www.cnn.com/2020/03/13/asia/china-coronavirus-us-lijian-zhao-intl-hnk/index.html.

Wong, Edward, and Julian E. Barnes. "U.S. Officials Push for Expelling Suspected Chinese Spies at Media Outlets." *New York Times*, March 26, 2020. https://www.nytimes.com/2020/03/26/us/politics/coronavirus-china-spies.html.

Wright, Thomas. "The Return to Great-Power Rivalry Was Inevitable." *The Atlantic*, September 12, 2018. https://www.theatlantic.com/international/archive/2018/09/liberal-international-order-free-world-trump-authoritarianism/569881.

PART FIVE: THE GATHERING STORM

Abdelmahmoud, Elamin (@elamin88). "I'd like to personally congratulate rich people, you did it again." Twitter post, May 14, 2020. https://twitter.com/elamin88/status/1261000691075727363.

Abraham, Carolyn. "Your Brain on COVID-19." *The Walrus*, June 18, 2020. https://thewalrus.ca/your-brain-on-covid-19.

Allen, John, Nicholas Burns, Laurie Garrett, Richard N. Haass, G. John Ikenberry, Kishore Mahbubani, Shivshankar Menon, et al. "How the World Will Look After the Coronavirus Pandemic." *Foreign Policy*, March 20, 2020. https://foreignpolicy.com/2020/03/20/world-order-after-coroanvirus-pandemic.

Armstrong, Laura. "Golf Courses Will Be Among the Recreational Sports to Get an Early Start After the COVID-19 Lockdown." *Toronto Star*, May 1, 2020.

Associated Press. "U.S. COVID-19 Deaths Reach 20,200, Surpassing Italy as Highest in the World." Canadian Broadcasting Corporation, April 11, 2020. https://www.cbc.ca/news/world/u-s-covid-19-deaths-highest-in-world-1.5529861.

Austen, Ian. "For Canada, Finding a Vaccine Will Only Be Part of the Equation." New York Times, May 8, 2020. https://www.nytimes.com/2020/05/08/world/canada/coronavirus-vaccine-timeline.html.

Beaumont, Peter, Lorenzo Tondo, and Kim Willsher. "Coronavirus: A Disease That Thrives on Human Error." The Guardian, March 7, 2020. https://www.theguardian.com/world/2020/mar/07/coronavirus-a-disease-that-thrives-on-human-error.

Bidder, Benjamin, Felix Bohr, Anna Clauß, Jürgen Dahlkamp, Ullrich Fichtner, Jan Friedmann, Annette Großbongardt, et al. "Attention Slowly Turns to the Mother of All Coronavirus Questions." Der Spiegel, March 27, 2020. https://www.spiegel.de/international/germany/what-next-attention-slowly-turns-to-the-mother-of-all-coronavirus-questions-a-853a559e-d454-41e2-b8f2-e8f2c8d5ca18.

Boessenkool, Ken, and Dan Robertson. "Could the Coronavirus Financial Crisis Lead to Another Populist Storm?" Maclean's, April 14, 2020. https://www.macleans.ca/opinion/could-the-coronavirus-financial-crisis-lead-to-another-populist-storm.

British Broadcasting Corporation. "Coronavirus: Senior Chinese Officials 'Removed' as Death Toll Hits 1,000." February 11, 2020. https://www.bbc.com/news/world-asia-china-51453848.

Buruma, Ian. "Why Are Americans Trying to Fight COVID-19 with Guns?" Globe and Mail, April 6, 2020. https://www.theglobeandmail.com/opinion/article-why-are-americans-trying-to-fight-the-war-against-covid-19-with-guns.

Camus, Albert. The Plague. Translated by Stuart Gilbert. New York, New York: Vintage, 1991.

Che, Claire, Dandan Li, Dong Lyu, and Rachel Chang. "China Sacrifices a Province to Save the World from Coronavirus." *Bloomberg*, February 5, 2020. https://www.bloomberg.com/news/articles/2020-02-05/china-sacrifices-a-province-to-save-the-world-from-coronavirus.

Chu, Jeff. "Against The Tide." *Fast Company*, October 14, 2013. https://www.fastcompany.com/3018621/against-the-tide.

Cohen, Patricia, and Tiffany Hsu. "'Rolling Shock' as Job Losses Mount Even with Reopenings." *New York Times*, May 14, 2020. https://www.nytimes.com/2020/05/14/business/economy/coronavirus-unemployment-claims.html.

Dahinten, Jan, and Matthias Wabl. "Germany Faces Backlash from Neighbors Over Mask Export Ban." *Bloomberg*, March 9, 2020. https://www.bloomberg.com/news/articles/2020-03-09/germany-faces-backlash-from-neighbors-over-mask-export-ban.

Dooley, Ben, and Makiko Inoue. "Testing Is Key to Beating Coronavirus, Right? Japan Has Other Ideas." *New York Times*, May 29, 2020. https://www.nytimes.com/2020/05/29/world/asia/japan-coronavirus.html.

Duclos, Jean-Yves. "Inside Ottawa's 'Light-Speed' Epidemic-Driven Overhaul." Interview by Paul Wells. *Maclean's*, March 23, 2020. https://www.macleans.ca/politics/ottawa/inside-ottawas-light-speed-epidemic-driven-overhaul.

Fisman, David. "The Paradox of Prevention: By Avoiding the Worst, We Remain Vulnerable to Future Waves of Disease." *Globe and Mail*, May 21, 2020. https://www.theglobeandmail.com/opinion/article-the-paradox-of-prevention-by-avoiding-the-worst-we-remain-vulnerable.

Gillis, Wendy. "I Got to Know Toronto Intimately Through Running. Now, It's How I'm Staying Connected to My City." *Toronto Star*, March 24, 2020. https://www.thestar.com/life/opinion/2020/03/24/i-got-to-know-toronto-intimately-through-running-now-its-how-im-staying-connected-to-my-city.html.

Globe and Mail. "How Canada Gave a Pandemic the Key to the Country's Nursing Homes." April 14, 2020. https://www.theglobeandmail.com/opinion/

editorials/article-how-canada-gave-a-pandemic-the-key-to-the-countrys-nursing-homes.

Gormley, Shannon. "The Folly of Hope During the COVID-19 Pandemic." *Maclean's*, April 8, 2020. https://www.macleans.ca/opinion/the-folly-of-hope-during-the-covid-19-pandemic.

Graham-Harrison, Emma. "Coronavirus: How Asian Countries Acted While the West Dithered." *The Guardian*, March 21, 2020. https://www.theguardian.com/world/2020/mar/21/coronavirus-asia-acted-west-dithered-hong-kong-taiwan-europe.

Greenwood, Michael. "Saliva Samples Preferable to Deep Nasal Swabs for Testing COVID-19." *Yale News*, April 24, 2020. https://news.yale.edu/2020/04/24/saliva-samples-preferable-deep-nasal-swabs-testing-covid-19.

Hessler, Peter. "Life on Lockdown in China." *New Yorker*, March 20, 2020. https://www.newyorker.com/magazine/2020/03/30/life-on-lockdown-in-china.

Hutson, Matthew. "The Quest for a Pandemic Pill." *New Yorker*, April 6, 2020. https://www.newyorker.com/magazine/2020/04/13/the-quest-for-a-pandemic-pill.

Irfan, Umair. "The Case for Ending the Covid-19 Pandemic with Mass Testing." *Vox*, April 13, 2020. https://www.vox.com/2020/4/13/21215133/coronavirus-testing-covid-19-tests-screening.

Jones, Dan. "Your True Self: The Future is a Foreign Person." *New Scientist*, April 19, 2017. https://www.newscientist.com/article/2127901-your-true-self-the-future-is-a-foreign-person.

Jones, Marc, Wayne Cole, and Scott Murdoch. "Stocks Tumble Again as Morgan Stanley Sees U.S. Economic Growth Plunging to 74-year Low on Coronavirus Crisis." *Reuters*, March 23, 2020.

Kelly, Annie. "Who Goes Alt-Right in a Lockdown?" *New York Times*, April 7, 2020. https://www.nytimes.com/2020/04/07/opinion/coronavirus-isolation-radicalization.html.

Kimmelman, Michael. "Going with the Flow." *New York Times*, February 13, 2013. https://www.nytimes.com/2013/02/17/arts/design/flood-control-in-the-netherlands-now-allows-sea-water-in.html.

Kretschmer, Fabian. "Did China's Authoritarianism Actually Help the Coronavirus Spread?" *Deutsche Welle*, May 2, 2020. https://www.dw.com/en/did-chinas-authoritarianism-actually-help-the-coronavirus-spread/a-52268341.

Kulish, Nicholas, Sarah Kliff, and Jessica Silver-Greenberg. "The U.S. Tried to Build a New Fleet of Ventilators. The Mission Failed." *New York Times*, March 29, 2020. https://www.nytimes.com/2020/03/29/business/coronavirus-us-ventilator-shortage.html.

Kupferschmidt, Kai, and Jon Cohen. "China's Aggressive Measures Have Slowed the Coronavirus. They May Not Work in Other Countries." *Science*, March 2, 2020. https://www.sciencemag.org/news/2020/03/china-s-aggressive-measures-have-slowed-coronavirus-they-may-not-work-other-countries.

Laplante-Beauchamp, Terrie. "Three Days of Death and Disorder: A Montreal Orderly's Diary From a Nursing Home's Coronavirus Outbreak." *Globe and Mail*, April 15, 2020. https://www.theglobeandmail.com/canada/article-three-days-of-death-and-disorder-a-montreal-orderlys-diary-from-a.

Lee, Hsien Loong. "The Endangered Asian Century." *Foreign Affairs*, July/August 2020. https://www.foreignaffairs.com/articles/asia/2020-06-04/lee-hsien-loong-endangered-asian-century.

Lepore, Jill. "What Our Contagion Fables Are Really About." *New Yorker*, March 23, 2020. https://www.newyorker.com/magazine/2020/03/30/what-our-contagion-fables-are-really-about.

MacGregor Marshall, Andrew. "Thai-König tyrannisiert Untergebene in Alpen-Hotel." *BILD*, April 14, 2020. https://m.bild.de/wa/ll/bild-de/privater-modus-unangemeldet-54578900.bildMobile.html.

McChrystal, Stanley, Tantum Collins, David Silverman, Chris Fussell. *Team of Teams: New Rules of Engagement for a Complex World.* New York: Portfolio, 2015.

Medaris Miller, Anna. "New Zealand Has No New Coronavirus Cases and Just Discharged Its Last Hospital Patient. Here Are the Secrets to the Country's Success." *Business Insider,* May 28, 2020. https://www.business-insider.com/how-new-zealand-beat-coronavirus-testing-tracing-trust-in-government-2020-5.

Meyer, Robinson. "There's One Big Reason the U.S. Economy Can't Reopen." *The Atlantic,* May 8, 2020. https://www.theatlantic.com/science/archive/2020/05/theres-only-one-way-out-of-this-mess/611431.

Ministry of Infrastructure and Water Management (Netherlands). "Ruimte voor de rivieren." Accessed June 3, 2020. https://www.rijkswaterstaat.nl/water/waterbeheer/bescherming-tegen-het-water/maatregelen-om-overstromingen-te-voorkomen/ruimte-voor-de-rivieren/index.aspx.

Morrow, Adrian, and Tamsin McMahon. "In the U.S., Coronavirus Is a Failure Decades in the Making. Is There Time to Do Better?" *Globe and Mail,* June 10, 2020. https://www.theglobeandmail.com/world/us-politics/article-americas-other-crisis-covid-19-is-a-failure-decades-in-the-making.

Osmundsen, John A. "'Elephant Repellent'" *New York Times,* January 2, 1988. https://www.nytimes.com/1988/01/02/opinion/elephant-repellent.html.

Packer, George, "We Are Living in a Failed State." *The Atlantic,* June 2020. https://www.theatlantic.com/magazine/archive/2020/06/underlying-conditions/610261.

Pew Research Center. "Public Trust in Government: 1958–2019." April 11, 2019. https://www.people-press.org/2019/04/11/public-trust-in-government-1958-2019.

Reichmann, Deb. "Trump Disbanded NSC Pandemic Unit That Experts

Had Praised." Associated Press, March 14, 2020. https://apnews.com/ce014d-94b64e98b7203b873e56f80e9a.

Resnick, Brian. "Why It's So Hard to See Into the Future of Covid-19." *Vox*, April 18, 2020. https://www.vox.com/science-and-health/2020/4/10/21209961/coronavirus-models-covid-19-limitations-imhe.

Schmemann, Serge. "The Virus Comes for Democracy." *New York Times*, April 2, 2020. https://www.nytimes.com/2020/04/02/opinion/coronavirus-democracy.html.

Shaw, Richard. "Trust in Government Is High in NZ, But Will It Last Until the Country's Elections Later in the Year?" *The Conversation*, April 13, 2020. https://theconversation.com/trust-in-government-is-high-in-nz-but-will-it-last-until-the-countrys-elections-later-in-the-year-135840.

Stephenson, Mercedes, Stewart Bell, and Andrew Russell. "Military Teams Raise Concerns About Conditions at Ontario Care Homes." May 26, 2020.

Stephenson, Mercedes, and Maryam Shah. "Troops in Long-Term Care Homes Raise Concerns About Management, Say Many Workers Doing Their Best." *Global News*, May 31, 2020. https://globalnews.ca/news/7007826/coronavirus-troops-long-term-care-homes.

South China Morning Post. "Not Letting the Facts Ruin a Good Story." Accessed June 11, 2020. https://www.scmp.com/article/970657/not-letting-facts-ruin-good-story.

Taleb, Nassim Nicholas. *The Black Swan: The Impact of the Highly Improbable*. New York, New York: Random House, 2007.

Taylor, Derrick Bryson. "How the Coronavirus Pandemic Unfolded: A Timeline." *New York Times*, June 9, 2020. https://www.nytimes.com/article/coronavirus-timeline.html.

Thompson, Dennis. "Saliva COVID Test Alternative to Deep Nasal Swab." *HealthDay News*, April 27, 2020.

Tong, Scott. "Countries Race to Limit, Ban Exports of Masks, Ventilators, Other Gear." *Marketplace*, March 30, 2020. https://www.marketplace.org/2020/03/30/countries-race-to-limit-ban-exports-of-masks-ventilators-other-gear.

Victoria University of Wellington. "Research Shows New Zealanders Trust Government More, Churches and Charities Less." June 11, 2018. https://www.wgtn.ac.nz/news/2018/06/research-shows-new-zealanders-trust-government-more,-churches-and-charities-less.

Wattie, James (@jameswattie). "Ontario: where your butler can come over, but not your mother." Twitter post, May 14, 2020. https://twitter.com/jameswattie/status/1261001138175909888.

Wells, Paul. "The Doomed 30-Year Battle to Stop a Pandemic." *Maclean's*, April 21, 2020. https://www.macleans.ca/news/world/the-doomed-30-year-battle-to-stop-a-pandemic.

Whipple, Chris. "What the CIA Knew Before 9/11: New Details." *Politico*, November 13, 2015. https://www.politico.eu/article/attacks-will-be-spectacular-cia-war-on-terror-bush-bin-laden.

Wilkes, Tommy, and Lawrence Delevingne. "Central Banks Deploy Record Sums to Break Financial Logjam, but May Need More." *Reuters*, March 23, 2020. https://www.reuters.com/article/us-health-coronavirus-markets-liquidity/central-banks-deploy-record-sums-to-break-financial-logjam-but-may-need-more-idUSKBN21A0EQ.

Woodward, Aylin, and Shayanne Gal. "One Chart Shows How Many Coronavirus Tests Per Capita Have Been Completed in 6 Countries. The US Has Finally Caught Up." *Business Insider*, April 20, 2020. https://www.businessinsider.com.au/coronavirus-testing-per-capita-us-italy-south-korea-2020-4.

Yakabuski, Konrad. "Canada's Senior-Care Crisis Has Been Long in the Works." *Globe and Mail*, April 15, 2020. https://www.theglobeandmail.com/opinion/article-senior-care-crisis-has-been-long-in-the-works.

Yang, Yuan, Nian Liu, Sue-Lin Wong, and Qianer Liu. "China, Coronavirus and Surveillance: The Messy Reality of Personal Data." *Financial Times*, April 2, 2020. https://www.ft.com/content/760142e6-740e-11ea-95fe-fcd274e920ca.

Yourish, Karen, K.K. Rebecca Lai, Danielle Ivory, and Mitch Smith. "One-Third of All U.S. Coronavirus Deaths Are Nursing Home Residents or Workers." *New York Times*, May 11, 2020. https://www.nytimes.com/interactive/2020/05/09/us/coronavirus-cases-nursing-homes-us.html.

Yu, Sun, and Xinning Liu. "Strain of Life Under Lockdown Sparks Divorce Surge in China." *Financial Times*, April 3, 2020. https://www.ft.com/content/11990ff0-c8f5-4f60-9b0a-be06324a4ddb.

Zhang, Feng. "Officials punished for SARS virus leak." *China Daily*, July 2, 2004.

ACKNOWLEDGEMENTS

This book is not only about a pandemic, it was also produced in one, on a break-neck schedule. I would like to thank my editor and publisher at Signal, Doug Pepper, and everyone at Penguin Random House Canada who helped bring this book to fruition: the copy-editor, Maryn Alberts; McClelland & Stewart's publisher, Jared Bland; the cover designer, Matthew Flute; the managing editor, Kimberlee Hesas; the typesetter, Sean Tai; and the proofreader, Tara Tovell.

My gratitude goes out to my agent, Rob Firing of Transatlantic, without whose tireless work and guidance this book would not be possible.

I thank as well the writers and researchers whose work I consulted, and the people in these pages who trusted me to tell their stories.

ABOUT THE AUTHOR

Ethan Lou's writing has appeared in the *Guardian*, the *Globe and Mail*, *Maclean's*, the *South China Morning Post*, the *Walrus*, and the *Washington Post*. He is the author of *Once a Bitcoin Miner: Scandal and Turmoil in the Cryptocurrency Wild West*. Lou is a former *Reuters* reporter and has served as a visiting journalist at the University of British Columbia. He travels, but also lives in Toronto.